Turning Our Hearts Back to God

A Woman's Guide to Self-love, Purpose and Purposeful Relationships!

Khadijah A. Brown

Scripture quotations marked (NIV) are taken from the Holy Bible, New International Version®,
NIV®. Copyright © 1973, 1978, 1984, 2011 by Biblica, Inc.™ Used by permission of Zondervan. All
rights reserved worldwide. www.zondervan.com

Scripture quotations marked (AMP) are taken from the Amplified Bible, Copyright © 1954, 1958,
1962, 1964, 1965, 1987 by The Lockman Foundation. Used by permission.

Scripture quotations marked NLT are taken from the Holy Bible, New Living Translation,
copyright © 1996, 2004, 2015 by Tyndale House Foundation. Used by permission of Tyndale
House Publishers, Inc., Carol Stream, Illinois 60188. All rights reserved.

Scripture quotations marked KJV are taken from the Holy Bible, King James Version. Cambridge
Edition: 1769; King James Bible Online, 2020. www.kingjamesbibleonline.org.

ISBN: 978-0-578-649801 (paperback)

Printed in the United States of America

Dedication

First and foremost, I want to thank my Lord and Savior Jesus Christ for saving me and giving me the strength to endure. I give you all the glory all the honor and all the praise!! Thank you, Lord, for setting me free!!! I am no longer a slave…. My relationship with you means more to me than silver and gold. Thank you for revealing my true identity!! I love you, Papa!!

To my daughter Kennedi! You are mommy's greatest blessing and I thank God for you every day. My prayer is that you learn from my mistakes and become the best version of yourself. Our bond is unbreakable. You've been rocking with me throughout my spiritual walk. I'll never forget the first time you said to me, "Mommy God looks at the heart, man looks at clothes and shoes" you were only 8-years old but wise beyond your years. You're my heart in human form, my latest, my greatest inspiration!! Mommy loves you beyond words!!

Thank you to my beautiful mother Charlene, your strength is something I will always admire. I know life hasn't always dealt you an easy hand but you took lemons and made lemonade! You're the strongest woman I know. The greatest gift you could have ever given me was telling me about Jesus at a young age. I've seen you at your lowest moments, but you remained faithful and continued to seek God even when you felt like giving up. I love you so very much and I'm so proud of the woman you're becoming. I'm honored to call you Mom.

To my father Larry L. Brown, I love and miss you so much Daddy! I know you're smiling down on me telling me to reach for the stars! You're the kindest man I've ever known, your spirit, gentleness, honesty and good nature have been embedded in me since a child. I pray my future husband is half the man you were. You've always inspired me to be honest, loving and caring! I take the many lessons you've taught me with me every day. I can still hear your voice saying "ease your head out of the lion's mouth, don't yank it out!" Your words of wisdom are timeless and are forever with me!

To my family and friends, thank you for taking this journey with me. It means so much to me!! I love you all so very much!!

~Khadijah Brown

Instagram: @khadijahbrown127
khadijahbrown.com

Contents

Preface

∞ ∞ ∞

"The thief cometh not, but for to steal, and to kill, and to destroy; I am come that they might have life, and that they might have it more abundantly" (John 10:10, KJV).

For as long as I can remember, I ran, ran from God; from relationship to relationship trying to fill the voids I had deep within. When I didn't find what I needed in relationships filled with lust not love, I ran to material possessions thinking they would make me happy. I felt like I was in limbo, a weird place I couldn't seem to escape. From the outside looking in I had the perfect life—my own house, car, and plenty of money, but I was dying inside!

Then my dad, my father, my friend unexpectedly passed away. I can't explain in words the pain or grief that filled my heart. I went through a deep depression. I ran to alcohol and drugs (marijuana) to numb the pain and escape my thoughts.

I remember like it was yesterday; I had drunk a whole bottle of wine and was up late smoking and roaming the halls. But the pain wouldn't go away, I couldn't seem to shake it!!

I cried out to the Lord, I said, "I can't do this anymore. If you don't help me, I'm going to lose my mind. I can't pretend that I'm ok. I can't pretend that I don't need you." I tried everything, relationships, drugs, parties, material possessions, career change. But none of these things filled the void I had deep in my heart.

The Lord led me to a scripture in the Bible, Mark 8:36, "For what does it profit a man if he gains the whole world but loses his soul." To the world I was successful but I was dying inside.

Religion says, you must be all put together to come to God. But relationship says, I will meet you right where you are and do the perfecting.

To my sister, my friend, God will meet you right where you are. It doesn't matter what you've done or how the world sees you. The only thing that matters is how God sees you and He has a plan for your life greater than anything you can imagine!!

"Daughters of Jerusalem, I charge you by the gazelles and by the does of the field: Do not arouse or awaken love until it so desires" (Song of Song 2:7, KJV).

∞ ∞ ∞

Chapter 1: Roots

∞∞∞

Roots are defined as "the basic cause, source, or origin of something."

In most cases, it speaks to our belonging to a place or society. When we see ourselves, we see our ancestors, culture and or the environment in which we were brought up. If we're not careful, our roots can hold us back from obtaining everything God has for us. The enemy of our soul likes to remind us of where we came from, when we start to believe we can obtain greatness. We identify our abilities with the history that holds no bearings to our future. We forget that God's in control of our destinies and has good plans for us. I can admit it's hard changing your mindset, when you've been surrounded by defeat and have never seen it done before.

God doesn't want us to identify our capabilities by our origin or the society in which we were brought up. He didn't place us in those environments to hold us back, but to show the world that He qualifies the unqualified.

"But God chose the foolish things of the world to shame the wise; God chose the weak things of the world to shame the strong" (1 Corinthians 1:27, NIV).

Our roots made us the people we were before we formed a relationship with Christ. It's very important to take inventory of where you are planting your roots. If you're rooting yourself in pleasing others, comparison, old habits and or the demands of society. You'll always be subjected to the opinions of others. We can't afford to be rooted in things that don't bear good fruit, we must be deeply rooted in Christ.

"They on the rock are they, which, when they hear, receive the word with joy; and these have no root, which for a while believe, and in time

of temptation fall away" (Luke 8:13, KJV).

If we're not rooted in Christ, we will find ourselves spiritually bankrupt; feeling unworthy and always spreading ourselves too thin to please others. This in most cases leads to bitterness and or resentment. It provides an open door for the enemy to come in and wreak havoc in our hearts and lives. When we are separated from God, we are not rooted in truth. When we are rooted in Christ, we excel, know our value and don't need the approval or validation from others. Christ establishes us in truth so we're not blown by the winds of life.

It wasn't until I formed a relationship with God that I begin to realize I had planted my roots in the wrong things.

My mother married my father at the age of nineteen while pregnant with me. My parents stayed married for ten-years, then divorced. I didn't understand nor was I able to comprehend the long-term effects the divorce had on me as a child. When you're a kid, you never get the opportunity to fully process what has happened until much later in life.

A few years later my mother remarried. My stepfather was a nice, loving and kind man, he always treated me and my siblings with love and care. I developed a relationship with him early on and he has played a major role in my life.

However, he and my mother were not good for each other. Looking back, I see they brought out the worst qualities in one another. Their inability to communicate caused a lot of problems in the home. Before I knew it, minor disagreements turned into explosive fights. I witnessed tables being broken, harsh words being spoken and bloodshed. This affected the way I viewed life and relationships. I became reserved and untrusting. I learned early on, this was the way to handle conflicts. When I became angry, I would behave in the same manner I witnessed as a child. I didn't understand where my temper and the negative emotions originated, until I looked back at my past.

When I hear people say, "that's just how I am," I understand what they mean. I learned that the person you perceive yourself to be is based on an idea that's not always true. The decisions from the past can dictate your future if you're not careful. There are attitudes and wrong beliefs that shaped that old person. Until you are healed and made whole every decision you make will be a representation of the pain. It isn't until our heavenly Father begins to shape and mold us, that we realize the people we were. Are so different from the women we will ultimately become. To grab hold of the opportunities God has for you, you must make peace with your past. You must see yourself the way God sees you. When we're rooted in Christ, the burdens from our pasts can no longer hold us back from our future. The thoughts and opinions of others no longer hold weight. We're no longer drawing from a barren well but drawing from the rivers of Living Water.

"For he shall be like a tree planted by the waters, which spread out its roots by the river, and will not fear when heat comes; but its leaf will be green, and will not be anxious in the year of drought, nor will cease from yielding fruit" (Jeremiah 17:8, KJV).

My parents did the best they could with what they knew. I am grateful to them for instilling principles such as honesty, love, accountability and the importance of having a relationship with God. My mother's Christian and my father was a Muslim. In any case, I learned a great deal from them both while watching their reverence for the Creator of the universe. I watched my Father pray several times a day. He would always tell me to "make sure to ask the Lord to look over me and keep me safe." I saw my mother at her weakest moments and the strength she embodied as a result of her dependency on God.

The decision my parents made to impart knowledge, awareness and reverence of God, has helped me to form a deeper relationship with my heavenly Father. My relationship with God has gotten me through some of the most devastating seasons in my life. Christ established me in truth and realigned me with the divine plans and purposes He had for my life. When we're deeply rooted in Christ, we can accept our real identity in Him. We can avoid the schemes of the enemy and let go of fear and false identities. Our cups will overflow and we will thrive. We won't be in search of validation from friends, family, or the world. We will be in divine alignment with our Creator and will bear good fruit in every season.

God is calling us to accountability, He wants to partner with us so His glory can be manifested on the earth. When we submit ourselves to God, He begins to work with us hand and hand. God will begin to align every decision we make so it's beneficial to our future legacy. This will teach us to discipline ourselves, so, we can see the bigger picture. Think about the impact you could have on future generations. Allow God to rewrite your story and embrace the new woman. Let go of the past and spend time with God so He can reestablish you by the rivers of Living Water. If you're holding onto anything that is not like God, such as anger, bitterness, regret, self-condemnation, pride or fear. Ask God to remove those things that are not like Him, so you can be rooted in truth.

∞∞∞

Chapter 2: Who Am I?

∞ ∞ ∞

"The Lord has made everything for its own purpose. Even the wicked for the day of evil" (Proverbs 16:4, AMP).

Many of us spend our whole lives not knowing who we really are. We allow our environment, ethnicity, social media, friends, family and our upbringing to determine who we can become. Deep down inside we aren't comfortable with the person we look at in the mirror every day. We know we're capable of more but have settled into mediocrity. We place our value in the temporary things of this world. The average woman can't tell you who she is outside of her worldly possessions.

When we begin to identify ourselves with what we do and what we have. We miss the mark! We become slaves to the systems of this world. We begin to compare ourselves to others, in attempts to emulate what we see on TV and social media. If you compare yourself to anyone, you're devaluing the unique qualities God has placed in you, as well as the other person. God doesn't create duplicates; you're one of a kind and wonderfully made by the hands of your heavenly Father.

The sun's purpose is to provide light, heat, and energy to the earth. We all have a divine purpose, we're not random. The authentic nature of who you are is within and was placed there by God before the beginning of time. We are made in the image of our heavenly Father who is the Creator of the universe. God has given us natural abilities and talents to create in the world.

"So, God created mankind in his own image, in the image of God he created them; male and female he created them" (Genesis 1:27, NIV).

The world tells us to be employees and not creators. But we were created in the image of God. We have a divine nature to create things that don't exist. The first thing God told Adam and Eve was to be fruitful and multiply. God the author and finisher of our faith has given each of us a gift that He wants us to serve to the world. God has given each of us a burden—an untapped area that only you have the grace to do. There may be something you witness within your community or country that breaks your heart; God may be calling you to this area to bring about change. In each of us are the solutions to the problems that affect our society the most. We have a responsibility as children of God to change the existing systems of this world and continue the advancement of the Kingdom of God.

In order to advance the Kingdom of God the body of Christ must be represented in every system of the world. The systems that currently exist in this world are part of a perverted system that was created by Satan. When we surrender our lives to Christ, He can use us as His vessels here on earth. When you build your relationship with your heavenly Father, He will begin to reveal things to you about yourself that you didn't know. The Holy Spirit will begin to uncover passions and gifts that have been lying dormant. These gifts and passions that you can't seem to shake are God given. They're a part of who you are and who God is calling you to be in this earth. It's your gift that will make room for you. You won't be truly fulfilled until you have established a relationship with your heavenly Father and are operating in your gift.

"The blessing of the Lord, it maketh rich, and he addeth no sorrow with it" (Proverbs 10:22, KJV).

God knows the desires of your heart; He put those desires there for His purposes. God gives all His children good gifts; it's our job to utilize those gifts to glorify our heavenly Father. Don't be afraid to explore your gifts and abilities.

To know yourself, you must first know your creator. When God formed you in your mother's womb, He had a plan for your life. Sometimes we allow the pain of our past, fear and mistakes to speak to our destiny. God is never puzzled by the happenings of your life. In His sovereignty, He designed everything for His own purposes. He knows, the environment you grew up in, the people who've hurt you and all the obstacles you've had to faced.

To know where you're going and who you will become, you must first know whose you are. Once you've established whose you are, you will be able to move freely. Knowing the work that has started in you will continue until Christ's second coming. Knowing whose you are is so important because you will face many trials and tribulations in this life. The only thing that will keep you stable is knowing who you belong to. When we know who we belong to, we move different and find strength in our Creator. It doesn't matter what kind of past you come from or what you've had to go through before getting to this point. Your new life is hidden in Christ. The person you were before you gave your life to Christ doesn't matter. You could've been a CFO for a major corporation or working for a local fast-food chain. When we surrender our lives to Jesus, the old people we were dies, so, our new lives can manifest.

"That ye put off concerning the former conversation the old man, which is corrupt according to the deceitful lusts; And be renewed in the spirit of your mind; And that ye put on the new man, which after God is created in righteousness and true holiness" (Ephesians 4:22-24, KJV).

The old ideas you entertained before Christ must die so you can become a new creature in Christ. You can't be afraid of what you may lose in the process of becoming who God created you to be. God is doing a new thing and He wants to prepare you for the things He has for you. When much is given, much is required. We are called to a higher standard and that requires our full obedience. We must allow the Creator to perfect us and remove the old mindsets and strongholds that have kept so many of us bound. If we don't allow our creator to show us who we are. We will believe the lies Satan tells us about ourselves based on past experiences. The enemy will tell you lies to keep you bound by shame and the mistakes of your past.

Christ wants us to walk in truth and know that our new life is in Him and not in our past. We're not our past experiences, mistakes, or disappointments. We're not what the world calls us. When we allow God to purge us, He begins to remove preconceived notions we have of ourselves and others.

As I look back, I realized early on I wasn't completely aware of whom I was as the daughter of the King. It wasn't until I begin to strengthen my relationship with God, that I begin to understand the woman God was calling me to be. God begin to reveal to me the things, He called me to do on earth. He also made me aware of some of the gifts He had given me. The Lord began to reveal areas in my life that He needed to purge. I had a lot of wrong ideas about myself and other people. There were words spoken against me as a child that left me feeling rejected and affected my confidence.

Words that are spoken against you in your youth can fester and take root. It can change the way you feel about yourself and see other people. When you aren't confident in who you are, you can allow others to define you and give you an identity that is not your own. They will assign a value to you and before you know it, someone else will be telling you what you can and can't do. There are so many things God has in store for you. But if you allow other people to assign a value to you based on their familiarity with you, you'll always try to live up to their expectations.

"A prophet is not without honour, but in his own country, and among his own kin, and his own house" (Mark 6:4, KJV).

Even Jesus, the Savior of the world, was assigned an identity that wasn't His own by the people in His hometown. The people became offended because He spoke with authority and had great wisdom. He also didn't follow specific Jewish customs. They were comfortable with the Jesus who hadn't fully stepped into His purpose but not the purpose driven Jesus, the Messiah. The people in His hometown lacked the faith to receive miracles.

Therefore, it's important to know who you are and whose you are. Also, ask God to give you the spirit to love like He does. You may be rejecting the miracle He wants to bring, because you've become too comfortable with the vessel.

God doesn't call the qualified, He qualifies the called. You don't have to be perfect for God to use you. God knows the sin you will commit next week and He still accepts you as His own. God wants to restore the woman you are now. He is outside of time, that means, He can go back and restore the 8, 18, or 30-year-old to her rightful place. It may have been bitter words spoken to you by a parent, caretaker, friend or significant other but at some point, those words have taken root and allowed you to stay stuck in the same place for years. God is the creator of all things including time, so, He's the only one who has the power to restore what has been lost.

"And I will restore to you the years that the locust hath eaten, the cankerworm, and the caterpillar, and the palmerworm, my great army which I sent among you" (Joel 2:25, KJV).

I'm thankful we serve a God who's in the restoration business. We're constantly evolving and becoming the women God is calling us to be. The Holy Spirit is always working in us to bring greater revelation and allow us to see the things that are not like Jesus. To fully understand and comprehend who we are, we must surrender our lives over to the will of God. When we surrender our lives to the will of God, He can remove the lies Satan has told us about ourselves. He can remove us from the Kingdom of this world.

"Do not conform to the pattern of this world but be transformed by the renewing of your mind. Then you will be able to test and approve what God's will is—his good, pleasing and perfect will" (Romans 12:2, NIV).

In Him, our new identity is revealed and old things have passed away. God doesn't want us to believe who the world says we are. He wants us to believe His word about us, which brings life and truth.

Your heavenly Father will meet you right where you are and began a good work in you. His desire is for you to follow Him and allow Him, to show you the woman He has called you to be. He wants you to understand how beautiful and special you are to Him. You're beautifully and wonderfully made and brought with a price. Don't allow anyone to tell you who you are based on anything external.

∞ ∞ ∞

∞∞∞

Naked is defined as bare, stripped, or destitute. Being in a place of complete vulnerability, a place that is unprotected and exposed.

"Trust ye not in a friend, put ye not confidence in a guide: keep the doors of thy mouth from her that lieth in thy bosom" (Micah 7:5, KJV). There are very few people in the world you can bear your soul to. It's hard opening up to people about painful memories. Like Adam and Eve, I hid myself from God. I thought I needed to be perfect before I formed a relationship with the Creator of the universe.

In the past, I was rejected when I showed my true self. I became quiet, reserved and untrusting. I never spoke about things that bothered me or caused me pain. I left all those emotions bottled up. It was as if I'd written everything that hurt me on a piece of paper and sealed it in a glass jar in my heart. I wanted to be accepted and loved, but I was met with false hopes from people whom I felt failed me. I didn't trust anyone with my heart or my true feelings. The same feelings I had for people, I associated with God.

You see, exposure makes it real; it forces you to deal with the open wound. When darkness is exposed to light, there is no way of hiding it. I didn't know I was running from the only one who understood me and had the power to heal me. God was gentle with me and helped me unpack all the ugly places my soul visited.

There is freedom in Christ and He wants a relationship with His daughters. Religion teaches, you must look a certain way or be put together to come to God. A true relationship with God shows you, it's not your job to change yourself. When we think we must be put together to come to God, we hide ourselves as Adam and Eve did in the Garden of Eden. Our heavenly Father knows our sinful nature.

"He knows our frame; He is mindful that we are dust" (Psalm 103:14, KJV).

He wrote the end before He wrote the beginning. He knows how you got to this place. He knows your inner wounds, the scars that no one can see. He doesn't expect you to save yourself but wants you to come to him with your broken pieces. He's the Potter, you're the clay.

"Are you so foolish? After beginning with the Spirit, are you now trying to attain your goal by human effort" (Galatians 3:3, NIV)?

When we attempt to do things in our own strength, it's of the flesh. This doesn't allow the fullness of God to dwell on the inside of us. God knows we don't have the capacity or the strength to change ourselves. He doesn't want you attempting to change yourself externally. He knows a transformation must take place within the heart. It's not by might, nor by power but by His spirit that we are set free in our mind, will and emotions.

God will meet you right where you are and clean you up from the inside out. God desires intimacy and honesty. He knows you're tormented by the pain of your past. He doesn't want you to hide from Him and run to the things of this world. He wants a relationship that's built on truth, He doesn't see you as the world sees you.

"And it came to pass, as Jesus sat at meat in the house, behold, many publicans and sinners came and sat down with him and his disciples. And when the Pharisees saw it, they said unto his disciples Why eateth your Master with publicans and sinners? But when Jesus heard that, he said unto them, they that are whole need not a physician, but they that are sick" (Matthew 9:10-12, KJV).

There are people in the body of Christ who operate out of a religious spirit just like the Pharisees. They pass judgment and want to tell you what your relationship with Christ should be. These individuals don't have a real relationship with Christ; they're bound by religious customs.

"Therefore, do not let anyone judge you by what you eat or drink, or with regard to a Sabbath day. These are a shadow of the things that were to come; the reality, however, is found in Christ" (Colossians 2:16-17, NIV).

If you've encountered this spirit inside or outside of the church, know this doesn't reflect the love God has for you. Our God calls you beautiful and He loves you with an everlasting love.

"My beloved spoke and said to me, Arise, my darling, my beautiful one, come with me" (Song of Songs 2:10, NIV).

Man looks at the outward appearance but God looks at the heart. God doesn't want us to come to Him prideful and put together. He knows we don't have the strength or the power to save ourselves or set ourselves free. Therefore, God gave His only begotten son Jesus to pay the price for our sinful nature. There's redemption in the blood of Christ and we're forgiven for our sins and transgressions. God wants our broken pieces. He wants to clean up the parts of us we're ashamed to show the world.

"Now why dost thou cry out aloud? Is there no king in thee" (Micah 4:9, KJV)?

As daughters of the King, we have the presence of the Lord within us. Our Creator doesn't want us wallowing in our sorrows or regrets. There's freedom in the presence of your heavenly Father. When we get naked with our Creator and bare our soul, we are reaffirmed in our relationship as daughters of the King. The enemy can no longer use our pasts to shame us and keep us in bondage. When you get naked with God, you're allowing your heavenly Father to heal those places where you hurt.

It requires honesty and vulnerability in every area of your life. You may be saying to yourself, God already knows everything I've done and all I've been through. You're correct. God does know all you've been through but for God to heal those areas of your past, you must open your heart. Our Father is a gentleman and won't come into any area that we don't invite Him into. God doesn't want our lip service; He wants our hearts.

"Keep thy heart with all diligence; for out of it are the issues of life" (Proverbs 4:23, KJV).

Our Creator is the only one who knows what resides in our hearts. He knows where every stronghold in your life stems from. He's not bound by time like we are. God is the Creator of time and seasons, and He holds each season of your life in His hands. He has the divine ability to go back into time and heal those old wounds. God doesn't want you burdened by past disappointments and setbacks.

When we expose our souls to the Creator of the universe, we're speaking our truth no matter how ugly and uncomfortable it is. We're stripping ourselves and allowing the Master potter to mold the clay to His satisfaction. We're opening our hearts and allowing God to restore those broken pieces we hid from others. These old wounds hold us back from the blessings God has for us.

Getting naked with God is a form of surrender. This gives our Creator the opportunity to remove any and everything that's not like Him. We're telling God every part of us that hurts, so, He can rebuild us and set us in our rightful place. To build a strong relationship with your heavenly Father, you must be honest with Him and come to Him with everything.

"For there is not a word on my tongue, but behold, O Lord, you know it altogether" (Psalm 139:4, KJV).

The Lord knows your quiet thoughts. He hears your voice when you speak, He knows the tears you've cried. Our heavenly Father doesn't sleep or slumber, He is always watching and listening. When you get naked with God, you're telling Him about everything that hurt you from childhood until now. You are speaking candidly to your Father about all your struggles and pains.

This will help you to form a more intimate relationship that's based on truth. God will give you the grace to forgive and let go of the things and people who hurt you. He will give you the ability to forgive yourself and release you from anger, bitterness, regret and self-condemnation. You'll be able to step fully into your new life.

The first time I got naked with God, I told Him about all the things that hurt me, words that were spoken against me as a child and the painful memories that still haunted me. As I bared my soul and I wept at the feet of Jesus, I felt years of shame, guilt, regret and fear instantly lift off me. The Lord began to impart love, confidence, wisdom, and understanding. The Father healed me of years of soulish wounds that the enemy used to torment me. Wounds that caused me to make decisions that weren't in my best interest.

"When a woman who had lived a sinful life in that town learned that Jesus was eating at the Pharisee's house, she brought an alabaster jar of perfume, and as she stood behind him at his feet weeping, she began to wet his feet with her tears. Then she wiped them with her hair, kissed them and poured perfume on them" (Luke 7:37-38, NIV).

The enemy wants us to stay stuck in our feelings because he knows it keeps us from moving forward with life. He knows a hurt Christian can't move in power and help deliver others. Satan is not afraid of religion, he's afraid of you forming an authentic relationship with Christ. He knows what happens when darkness is exposed to light. He doesn't want you to operate in authority and power. He wants your prayers to be aligned with fleshly desires and not the will of the Father.

"One day the evil spirit answered them, Jesus I know, and I know about Paul, but who are you" (Acts 19:15, NIV)?

When we're bogged down by the past, we aren't operating in our kingdom authority. The enemy uses idols to give us a false sense of security. An idol is something that a person worships.

Some people idolize fame, fortune, food, sex, drugs/alcohol, other people, and material possessions. Idols are used to numb the pain but they don't fix the problem. The enemy tricks us into thinking these idols will fix the problem but instead they create deeper voids in the human soul.

These things distract us from God's real purpose for our lives. The temporary idols that we seek will only cause more pain and anguish and take us out of alignment with the Father. Only the Creator of our souls can reach in and heal the pains of the past. You can't sex it away, drink it away, smoke it away, or spend it away.

The enemy doesn't want you set free. He wants you to feel guilty and live in self-condemnation for sins God has already forgiven you for. He wants you to hide from the presence of God, so you can remain in darkness. He wants you to believe that God is upset with you, so, you can stay in a shameful place. The enemy uses religious people to shame you and keep you from the presence of God.

"When the Pharisee who had invited him saw this, he said to himself, if this man were a prophet, he would know who is touching him and what kind of woman she is that she is a sinner" (Luke 7:39, NIV).

It's a lie!!

God can use everything that the devil meant for bad for His glory. The Lord is the only one who has the power to bring restoration, mend broken hearts and forgive us for our sins.

"Therefore, I tell you, her many sins have been forgiven for she loved much. But he who has been forgiven little loves little" (Luke 7:47, NIV).

In the book of Genesis, Ch 37, we learn about the life of Joseph, he was the son of Jacob (Israel). His siblings were jealous and hated him because of the love he received from his father and the dreams God had given him. One day some of his brothers conspired to kill him but later decided to sell him into slavery.

"Judah said to his brothers, What will we gain if we kill our brother

and cover up his blood? Come, let's sell him to the Ishmaelites and not lay our hands on him; after all, he is our brother, our own flesh and blood" (Genesis 37:26-27, NIV).

God allowed Joseph to be sold into slavery, so, he would be in direct alignment with his purpose. You see, Joseph didn't know the process God would take him through to receive the promise. Everything the enemy meant for bad, God used for His glory. Our heavenly Father's desire is to set the captives free and remove any painful memory that keeps us from moving forward. To get free you must get in the presence of your heavenly Father and speak your heart. That means coming clean about your true feelings, no matter how ugly or painful they may be.

"And Joseph made haste; for his bowels did yearn upon his brother: and he sought where to weep; and he entered into his chamber, and wept there" (Genesis 43:30, KJV).

Joseph was so overwhelmed with emotion, that he needed to go to the secret place and weep, so, God could release all the hurt, pain and bitterness he felt toward his brothers over the years. He wouldn't be able to move forward if he hadn't opened his heart to God. Joseph went from the prison to the palace and he was able to forgive and help his family when the land was under famine. There are times, we must endure hardships we don't understand. When we give these things to God, He can give us the right perspective and use it for His glory.

You like me may have tried everything and nothing has seemed to fill the void you have within. I challenge you to get naked with God and form an intimate relationship that is built on truth. God doesn't want you performing religious activities. He wants an authentic relationship!!

∞ ∞ ∞

∞∞∞

Many young women grow up wondering, who they'll marry, when they'll marry and at what age they'll marry. We have our hearts set on how old we want to be and if we've started dating, we're normally mesmerized or captivated by our first love believing it will last forever. In most cases, we're unaware of the heartbreak we'll experience, the let downs and the unhealthy choices we'll make in many relationships. We don't understand that these relationships are temporary and won't last forever.

I was 17 years old when I experienced my first heartbreak. Shortly after graduating high-school, I was smitten by this one fellow who was way too old for me. You see this guy was ten-years my senior, which means he was 27. At the time, I believed I was mature enough to handle a relationship of this caliber. I saw young girls dating older men all the time in my neighborhood. This was considered the norm where I grew up. As I look back and reflect on the nature of the relationship, I can see now, I'd been taken advantage of by a much older man. My mindset wasn't developed nor was I ready to experience any kind of romantic love.

I was naïve and didn't have the knowledge nor the experience to be dating someone that much older. I can't say, I was in love because I wasn't. I was young, inexperienced, curious and a virgin. I didn't date much in high school; this was brand new for me. I had never had a serious relationship, a high school sweetheart or was one of those girls you would consider "fast" or "fresh" as the elders would say. But little did I know the same pain that introduced those girls to the fast/fresh lifestyle led me to date a much older man. Pain speaks its own language depending on the person inflicted by the pain.

As the months quickly passed; I found myself giving one of my most prized possessions to a man whom I thought cared for me. I found out a few days later how much he cared. I received a phone call from a young lady stating she was dating the same man I'd just lost my virginity to. I never spoke to him or saw him again. I didn't have the strength to confront him or speak candidly about my feelings to anyone. I had a lump in my throat that would not go away. It stayed there longer than I can remember. I wished I could turn back the hands of time and wish this whole ordeal away but there was no way to escape the pain or the shame that confronted me daily.

I was crushed beyond words......

I didn't understand why this had happened to me and I blamed myself over and over as I replayed the events in my head. "How could I be so foolish? Why was I so trusting?"

Little did I know, I wasn't ready for a relationship and didn't have the right relationship with God. My feelings of neglect and loneliness, allowed me to enter a relationship in my youth with someone I believed would provide validation. I wasn't whole and I never took the time necessary to heal from my past.

As I grew older, I begin to develop unhealthy habits that aided in my choosing the wrong relationships. Time and time again, I continued to pursue relationships that weren't good for me. I thought it was the men I'd encountered, never realizing I had internal issues I hadn't dealt with since childhood. I couldn't identify what was good for me and I didn't understand my worth as the daughter of the King.

The Lord revealed that I suffered from abandonment issues that stemmed from childhood. I struggled with rejection and this affected the way I made decisions. I carried the pain from my past and continuously made wrong decisions giving of myself in relationships that I thought were built on love but in all actuality, they were lustful in nature. The foundation of these relationships wasn't solid. I didn't know how to love myself, so I settled for less then I deserved. I wasn't aware of the internal pain that guided my decisions, so I moved mindlessly without the direction of God.

This pathway led to destruction and cost me more than I gained. I was left feeling empty, broken, ashamed, and insecure. I lived in self-condemnation for as long as I could remember. I tore myself apart focusing on the shame and guilt from my past. Painful relationships and words spoken against me haunted me daily.

I thought that God could never love me because of all the things I'd done. One day while reading my Bible, the Lord placed this scripture on my heart and it brought freedom.

"Fear not; for thou shalt not be ashamed; neither be thou confounded; for thou shall not be put to shame; for thou shalt forget the shame of thy youth, and shalt not remember the reproach of thy widowhood anymore" (Isaiah 54:4, KJV).

In this moment, I felt kissed by God. He reminded me that even when I'm at my lowest point and everyone has left. He is right there with me in the trenches wiping the tears and reminding me of His eternal love and faithfulness.

We've all made mistakes and fallen short of the glory of God. All you need to do is ask for forgiveness and allow God to come into your heart and remove anything that keeps you bound by your past. When you open your heart to God; He can reveal and heal those areas in your heart that affect your decisions. Ask him to expose the hidden idols, the things you use to numb the pain of the past. If you've fallen into sexual immorality, ask God to take the desires away and fill the voids deep within your heart.

When I rededicated my life to Christ. The Holy Spirit began to reveal the soulish wounds that kept me in bondage. I was a slave to sexual sin and tried many times to stop. I asked the Lord to "remove any spirit in me that kept me bound to sexual immorality". This wasn't a one-day prayer. I had to continually sit at the feet of Jesus and ask him to change the way I thought.

I used to think that if I was in a relationship, it was ok to have sex. The spirit of lust kept me bound. I felt obligated based on the relationship status to continually give of myself sexually. I had the wrong idea about love and relationships. In His presence, the Lord showed me that any relationship I entertained would be unhealthy because I wasn't whole. I was looking for someone to fill those broken pieces, never knowing that they would never be able to fill my empty spaces. The men I chose were just as broken as me. I didn't know it but I was longing for an encounter with Jesus.

Our God is not sitting in Heaven condemning us for our failures or mistakes. He loves us with an everlasting love and promises to restore everything that we have lost. When you have established a relationship with God, the Holy Spirit is able to come into your heart and remind you of His plans. Our heavenly Father wants us to come to Him with everything, unlike people He can handle the good and bad parts of us. The Lord was able to strip every lie the enemy told me about myself and begin to reveal truth.

In His presence, I was refreshed and made new. Jesus wiped the slate clean and forgave me for all my sins. It doesn't matter what you've done our Heavenly Father has the power to make all things new in your life. God uses every pain, sorrow and grief for His glory and your story will be a testimony of His power.

Jesus suffered so we could be free. Your suffering will not be in vain but will be used to glorify your heavenly Father.

"Yet it pleased the Lord to bruise him; he hath put him to grief: when thou shalt make his soul an offering for sin, he shall see his seed, he shall prolong his days, and the pleasure of the Lord shall prosper in his hand" (Isaiah 53:10, KJV).

∞ ∞ ∞

∞∞∞

"The graveyard is the richest place on earth, because it is here that you will find all the hopes and dreams that were never fulfilled, the books that were never written, the songs that were never sung, the inventions that were never shared, the cures that were never discovered, all because someone was too afraid to take that first step, keep with the problem, or determined to carry out their dream."
– Les Brown

Millions of people die each year never knowing why God created them. They never take the necessary steps to explore their full potential and walk fearlessly in their purpose. In our adolescence, we have the confidence necessary to accomplish any goal we put our mind to. The first steps of a young child illustrate the boldness we're born with. We feel there is no mountain too high or obstacle too big that will keep us from following the desires of our hearts.

As we grow older, failure, regret, and disappointment set in and we lose our confidence in our abilities. Those same dreams and aspirations we saw ourselves doing in our youth leave us terrified. We're afraid of the unknown, so we lack the ability to prepare and press forward to something new. Our environment speaks louder than our dreams and many find it hard to escape the pain of the past. We are afraid to step out on faith because we've never seen anyone in our families be successful. We have only been exposed to the failures of our past and they speak louder than our dreams. Our inner voice doesn't speak to our potential only the things we've seen growing up, so we walk by sight and not by faith!

The opportunities and resources within my community didn't leave much hope or passion for the dreamer. I'd never seen anyone in my family start a business, graduate college or pursue something outside of the traditional 9 to 5 job. As a first-generation college graduate, I learned first-hand the unique difficulty of aspiring for something more, especially when all you've seen is poverty. I don't necessarily look at the struggles I've faced as a setback but rather a way in which God built resilience within me. I didn't allow the neighborhood I grew up in nor my family background to dictate what was possible for me.

When we allow our environment and past mistakes to speak to us, we allow a different version of ourselves to govern our actions. If we're not properly rooted in the word of God, we will allow fear and or our environment to rule our lives. The enemy of our souls wants us to stay in bondage and be cursed with fear; mimicking generations of brokenness and poverty.

"But perfect love drives out fear, because fear has to do with punishment. The one who fears is not made perfect in love" (1 John 4:18, KJV).

Your heavenly Father doesn't want you to live in fear. He has given you the strength to overcome any obstacle that stands in your way. You and I are overcomers!!

The times have changed and many are racking up thousands of dollars in student loan debt only to find shortly after graduation they hate the career they chose. It's important to always allow God to lead you into whatever career path you decide. I went to school for computer science because I believed, I would make a good living. But hindsight is 20/20 and had I known then what I know now, I would have pursued a different career path early on. In our youth, we're impressionable. We find ourselves following in the footsteps given to us by our family, friends, and society. Growing up, all I heard from my parents was "go to school, get a good job." I don't blame them because when they grew up, times were different and the only thing they hoped for were good jobs with the city or a company with longevity.

I watched my father work for the Budd Company for over thirty-three years. When he retired, all he got was a pension that was barely enough to cover the expenses he had accumulated over the years. When he passed away, I didn't recall seeing any of his bosses or co-workers at the funeral paying their respects. I worked for a company for over six years and when I was diagnosed with cancer, I didn't receive one card or visit from anyone within the company.

We spend all this time at these companies giving them the best parts of ourselves and we're just another employee ID. We spend the best part of our day at jobs we aren't satisfied with and keep us unhappy. When we get home, we're too tired and mentally drained to do anything that will benefit us or our families long-term. So, we settle for dinner and our favorite TV show never realizing we're distracted. We're literally watching our lives pass us by, refusing to use our God given gifts to create solutions that don't exist in the world. Our heavenly Father has called us to share our gifts with the world to bring about change and influence future generations. The rat race keeps us bound and distracted from following the true purpose God has for us. We are slaves to the system just like the Israelites were in Egypt. When God tried to remove them from that system, they were reluctant and desired to go back into bondage.

We like comfort and security; we abandon anything that makes us step outside our comfort zone. Either we're chasing money or stability but the outcomes are always the same. We allow life to pass us by without ever actualizing all the promises God has for us. The society we live in tells us to work hard, go to college, get good paying jobs and work until retirement age. I'm not saying anything is wrong with college or a job, but if God has given you a dream, be intentional and pursue it. Don't give up on your dreams or allow circumstances or people to tell you what's not possible. Follow your heart and go with your God given passions, they will never deceive you. Don't follow the crowd and worry about money or material possessions, those things will come. Focus on God and allow the Holy Spirit to lead you to your destiny.

"For what will it profit a man if he gains the whole world and forfeits

his soul? Is anything worth more than your soul" (Matthew 16:26, AMP)?

The Lord took me to this scripture one day and spoke to me clearly. He showed me how I had traded my purpose for the things of this world. I had lost sight of God's purpose and plans for my life. I had forgotten what I liked and I wasn't operating in my gifts. I had essentially gained the world and lost my soul. As I look back, I realize everything I did at that time outside of Christ was meaningless. Solomon says, in Ecclesiastes 2:11, "Then I looked on all the work that my hands had wrought, and on the labour that I had labored to do and, behold, all was vanity and vexation of spirit, and there was no profit under the sun." Anything you do outside of God and your purpose is meaningless.

"But seek ye first the kingdom of God, and his righteousness; and all these things shall be added unto you" (Matthew 6:33, KJV).

It doesn't matter how much money you make or how successful you are in the world; it means nothing to God. Only the things of God are eternal. I thank God for restoring me and giving me vision, wisdom, and strength to step out on faith and follow my purpose. The Lord wants to set His daughters on fire with purpose and birth something new through us. We must be willing to step out on faith.

I've had a passion for acting my entire life. I would watch movies and emulate the characters I saw on TV. Despite my love for acting, I never pursued it in my youth. Acting in my community and family was considered a pipe dream. A career that was unattainable, so, I never took it seriously. I always thought, in the back of my mind, one day. But I never stepped out on faith because of my fear of failing. I never thought it was possible for someone in my community to be successful in acting. I figured if I pursued the careers that were considered safe, I wouldn't have to worry about failing. I wanted to fit in and never wanted to risk being an outcast. I knew I was good at Information Technology, so I followed a career that would pay well and I chose money over passion.

For years, I worked for corporations doing work I wasn't passionate about. If the money was right, I would commit, put my passion aside, and work. As the years quickly passed, I lost sight of myself and only cared about moving up the corporate ladder. I was depressed. Although other factors added to my depression. I couldn't help but think of all the things I'd lost sight of; I lost myself in the process of gaining material possessions. I never considered myself to be a materialistic person. But my lack of direction and focus on God had me chasing careers and not purpose. When I finally reached my breaking point, I knew there was no amount of money that would keep me in a career for twenty years that I wasn't happy with.

One day while praying and meditating on the word of the Lord. I begin asking the Lord what it was that still interests me. My first thought was acting; I said to myself, "You can't act. You're too old and it will take you forever to get in the industry." As I begin to doubt my abilities and talents, I heard the voice of the Holy Spirit say, "Who told you these things?" I knew at that moment they were lies from Satan. The enemy can't stop the plans and purposes of God for our lives. However, he can distract us and defeat us in our minds so we live in fear and never pursue God's promises. I'm thankful God didn't allow Satan to have the last say, He reminded me of who I was in Him. Two weeks later, I started acting classes, six months later, I got my first role in a short film. When I stepped out on faith and allowed God to be God. He moved in a supernatural way and opened doors of opportunity. When we step out on faith and trust God, there is a freedom and joy of knowing everything will be alright. I had to believe God could change my circumstances and He did. As women of God, we can't be afraid to step out on faith.

"Behold, I am the Lord, the God of all flesh. Is anything too difficult for Me" (Jeremiah 32:27, KJV)?

When God gives you a vision, He has the responsibility

of making that thing manifest in your life. God's word can never come back void. His promises are eternal but require active participation from the vessel. It's our responsibility to be steadfast, unmovable, and unshakeable. When we put all our trust in God, we're free to move when He tells us to move. When we're caught up in the trappings of this world. We can't operate in our full potential and be everything God has called us to be. God must get us to a place where our faith in Him out weights the circumstances that we find ourselves in. When the two meet we can make the bold moves and have bigger expectations of the Almighty God.

"Whosoever therefore shall humble himself as this little child, the same is greatest in the kingdom of Heaven" (Matthew 18:4, KJV).

When Jesus spoke in this parable, He was speaking of the childlike faith needed to follow Him. Jesus was telling the disciples that following Him required them to be fully submitted to the purpose He had for their lives, without knowing the full scope. When children follow their parents, they don't know what they'll eat, where they'll live or where they'll go. A good parent will always do what's best for the child, even when the child is uncomfortable.

When my daughter was small, she loved her pacifier. It was the only thing at times that would relax her and keep her quiet. Shortly after she turned one, I begin to wean her off the pacifier to avoid damaging her teeth. For several nights she cried uncontrollably and it was extremely hard to get her to sleep. I knew she was uncomfortable and I didn't like to hear her cry, but I knew what was best for her.

We may not understand the process but we must trust God and know, He will always do what's best for us. When we're humble as a child, we can allow the Holy Spirit to lead us to our purpose. To be humble as a child; we must be willing to step out on faith and risk falling knowing that our Heavenly Father will be there to guide us. It's knowing that the God who created you knows exactly what He has placed down on the inside of you. It requires a full surrender so something new can be birthed through you.

God doesn't want us pulling from our experiences and what we know. He wants us to step out on faith and surrender all. When we're a submitted vessel, He can operate freely through us and use us for His glory. There is confidence in knowing everywhere your foot may tread your heavenly Father has already made the provisions necessary for you to prosper.

"Before I formed you in the womb, I knew you, and before you were born, I set you apart" (Jeremiah 1:5, KJV).

God knew us when we were spirits before He wrapped us in flesh. That means, before He sent you to earth, He knew everything you would go through and He still chose you. God wants you to step into your destiny and be everything He has called you to be. He doesn't want you to be afraid to step out on faith.

Take a moment and think of something that you have always wanted to do but were too afraid to do. Write down the things you're most passionate about. Allow yourself to explore the possibilities of you doing that thing or following that dream.

The trail blazers of this world refused to allow what they had in their hands to dictate who they could become. The circumstances may not always be right but if you allow God to lead you, He will direct your path. Spend time with the Creator of your soul; He will reveal your purpose for creation.

∞ ∞ ∞

Chapter 6: God's Cry

∞∞∞

God has placed the desire to love and be loved in our hearts but warns us several times not to awaken love until the time is right. "Daughters of Jerusalem, I charge you by the gazelles and by the does of the field: Do not arouse or awaken love until it so desires" (Song of Songs 2:7, KJV). This scripture is mimicked throughout Song of Songs and it's God's cry to His daughters. You can see and feel the heart of God in His word. God is warning His daughters of the perceived dangers associated with the context. God knows what will happen when we rush into relationships, we're not ready for. He wants to help us avoid the pitfalls many women make in romantic relationships.

Many times, as women we move without the divine knowledge of our Creator. We love deeply and are nurturers by nature. We will always go the extra mile even when the relationship is not beneficial to us mentally, emotionally or physically. I can admit, I made a lot of bad decisions in relationships. I craved instant gratification, comfort and security but at my lowest moments, I still felt alone and unfulfilled.

As I look back and reflect on my own disobedience, I am reminded that even in that time God was with me. I never thought it would happen to me. I knew my mother, grandmother, friends and family had experienced it but I never thought it would hit so close to home. I didn't listen to the still small voice; the warnings God had given me. The verbal abuse and possessive nature spoke loudly but I didn't listen. I was twenty-three years old the first time a man had ever put his hands on me. I received a message from a young woman claiming she and the father of my unborn child were intimate several times. I was four months pregnant and had already experienced verbal abuse from my significant other. I can't explain in words the hurt, frustration and sadness that filled my soul at that moment.

I felt betrayed, lost, confused and in utter disbelief. I couldn't believe a man who claimed to love me could be so disrespectful and irresponsible. Not only with my life but the life of our unborn child. When I confronted him about the situation, he blew it off. I told him that the relationship was over. At that moment, he snapped and turned into a totally different person! I honestly don't think he was aware of his demeanor or the person he had become. He backhanded me and begin choking and pinning me down. I was completely caught off guard and emotionally and physically traumatized. I tried to fight back but had little strength. I remember praying silently asking the Lord to get me out of that situation.

All I could muster was a scream, "HELP ME"!!!" as tears rolled down my face. I thought I was going to die. I'm thankful the Lord heard my cry and had mercy on me.

God loves us and wants to protect us from the sorrow and pain we will experience in unhealthy relationships. He knows that two people that aren't whole can never come together and have a healthy relationship. I didn't realize it at the time, but I was broken and all my decisions were made from a broken place.

This terrible ordeal brought back so many bad memories from my childhood. My mother and stepfather had a volatile relationship; they constantly argued and fought. I remember there were times when the fights got so bad that broken glass would fill the floor in my home and everything would be in a disarray. This bothered me a lot growing up and I didn't trust men. I also developed a very bad temper that was explosive when ignited. I was afraid to be vulnerable and I built up a wall, I never trusted anyone beyond the surface. There were so many people in my life that claimed they loved each other, but the way they treated one another scared me. I figured, if this was love, I wanted no part of it. I didn't allow anyone to penetrate the wall I had put up. I used my silence and temper to protect my most vital possession, my heart.

I didn't want my daughter to see the same things I'd experienced as a child. I asked the Lord to remove him from my heart, so, I could walk away from the relationship. Forgiveness was a big part of this process. At one point, I felt so angry and bitter it consumed me and I couldn't get pass this offense. I prayed and ask the Lord to remove the painful emotions from the bad memories. The Lord showed me that hurt people, hurt people and how our actions reflect our many experiences. I didn't know at the time but my daughter's father was battling his own inner demons. He had issues that he hadn't dealt with just like me.

The Lord allowed me to see him and the situations I'd encountered in a different light and offer love and forgiveness. The person I saw that day was not the man God created. That wasn't who he was as a person, that behavior was learned. I could no longer view him from angry, bitter eyes, I had to view him through the eyes of love. God helped me to forgive him and forgive myself. When we don't forgive, the enemy can use those old memories to torment us. He can keep us bound and stuck in the past and unable to see the future. I understand now that forgiveness is for you and not necessarily for the other person.

I learned only Jesus can heal and set you free from the pain of your past. The pain of our past is hidden in our poor decisions and relationship choices. We want to be loved so much, that we will settle for the person right now and not the person we know we deserve. We make serious decisions from a place of brokenness, heartache, loneliness and pain. Making decisions from these places carry life altering consequences. I'm thankful the Lord gave me the strength to walk away from an emotionally and physically abusive relationship. But I can't forget the countless women that never find the strength to walk away.

When God brings a relationship together, it's for His divine purpose. Relationships that are God ordained will never cause physical or emotional pain. Relationships that are God ordained will bear fruit and edify. The man that God places in your life will serve a purpose. He will build you up, not tear you down. Some of the men we encounter have never had a touch from Jesus so they don't know or understand how to love the women in their lives. For a man to love you how Christ loved the church, he must have an intimate relationship with the Father and understand the importance of the rib. When he develops this relationship with God. He will learn how to love you more and create an environment that helps you thrive.

God wants to reveal the kind of mate He has for us through His love. Many of us don't really know what love is and have never experienced real love. God doesn't want us to get involved with relationships until we have begun the healing process. When we choose relationships from a broken place, we don't use discernment. When you're broken and feel empty you will run from relationship to relationship, hoping the next one will treat you right. The men you meet when you're hurting will never be able to fill the voids of your heart. Those voids can only be filled by the love of God. God knows all the tears you've cried. He knows the deep dark feelings about ourselves that we hide from the world. He knows all about the painful childhood memories and the unhealthy habits that have affected our families for generations.

God wants us to fall in love with Him and know how much He loves us. When you understand how much the Creator loves you, it can help you to navigate all relationships in your life. You will begin to view every relationship through the eyes of love. I have always loved God but wasn't able to comprehend how much He loved me. It's impossible to grasp the love God has for His children. If we knew how much God loved us, we would never settle for mediocrity. The love of God destroys strongholds and brings restoration. The love of God is so powerful, it overwhelmed me!! Everything I searched for my whole life was wrapped up in Him. The void that I carried since childhood was finally filled with the love of God. God's love teaches you to learn and love yourself. You can never fully love yourself or anyone else, until you realize how much the Creator loves you.

God desires intimacy with us more than we know. When we're intimate with the Creator, He can reveal things in us that we are unaware of. You won't know who you are until you're fully acquainted with the Creator. When you spend time in His presence reading the Bible, the word refreshes you and brings life.

Allow the Holy Spirit to direct your path and lead you to all truth. The man God has ordained for you will have the capacity to pour into you in every season of your life. God will raise up a man that will compliment you five, ten, twenty years down the line. God knows where you're going and where you've been.

∞∞∞

Chapter 7: The Culture

∞ ∞ ∞

Culture is defined as the quality in a person or society that arises from a concern for what is regarded as excellent in arts, letters, manners and scholarly pursuits.

Many of us long for someone we can share our scars and broken pieces with. Someone who will still be around flaws and all. We all desire that kind of love; the love that touches you when you feel like you can't be touched. The joy that hits you when you're in your darkest hour. One day, I was watching an old Eartha Kitt interview and she said something that hit me like a ton of bricks but resonated with me so well. She said, "A man has always wanted to lay me down, but he never wanted to pick me up." I could tell by the desperation in her voice she was longing for an encounter with someone that would accept her for who she truly was outside of the sexual nature she possessed as a woman.

This statement made me think of how many women grow up thinking that they aren't good enough to be loved only physically desired. "The culture" will have you believing that you must be over-exposed in every way to be desired by a man. Not knowing "the culture" not only leaves you exposed physically and emotionally but also tormented by the painful memories of feeling like you were never enough. We're taught by society to be sexual beings and many believe that's the only way to get close to a man. We're pressured into thinking that our bodies are the most important thing we have going for ourselves. We forget that God created us in His image and in His likeness. This means we have more to offer than our bodies.

The Bible says, "He who finds a wife finds what is good and receives favor from the Lord" (Proverbs 18:22, KJV). We are the good thing that the word of God is referring too. We aren't supposed to be in search of a man. He is supposed to be in search of us.

The culture doesn't teach young women that their bodies are temples and that only the man God has ordained for them to marry should see those intimate areas. No one tells you how these lustful relationships will leave you bruised, scarred, and feeling unworthy. As I look back and reflect, I can see what I thought was love was camouflaged as lust. I was influenced by the culture, the culture that glorifies premarital sex but doesn't speak about the children out of wedlock, sexually transmitted diseases, terminated pregnancies, heartbreak, deadly soul ties and emotional trauma.

I'm not speaking on an issue I know nothing about. This is an issue that I'm all too familiar with. I've had many relationships over the years that amounted to nothing but heartbreak and anguish. I was left picking up the pieces and bringing them back to God, so he could make sense of all my dysfunction and put me back together. I'm thankful that everything the devil meant for evil God uses for His glory. I pray I can impart some wisdom based on my experience and the knowledge I've received while being in the presence of God.

Women in our society have been brainwashed into thinking that their value is in their looks or in their womanhood. We find our confidence in the people that accept us. But finding your worth in people will never be enough. When you search for validation in relationships, you will find yourself in dark places. You will run to everyone who accepts you, whether good or bad. These men will feed off your need for validation and will use your body to fulfill their fantasies. You will think that any rejection you receive reflects your worth. You will give of yourself endlessly trying to please people that were never meant to stay in your life. As women, we're always willing to adapt to please our mates. Always willing to go the extra mile, even when we're in relationships that don't speak to who we are. We allow men who don't have pure intentions to define us. God never intended for another human being to validate you.

God created you and knows all that He has placed down on the inside of you. He would never allow another person to put His creation in a box of unworthiness, fear, and self-doubt. That's not the fruit of being children of God. That's the perverted system of the enemy. His goal has always been to kill, steal, and destroy God's creation. Over the years, I've been in some toxic relationships. When you don't deal with the pain, you limit your level of expectations and what you feel you deserve. There are relationships you form when you're not your best self. These relationships are toxic and don't speak to the woman God has called you to be. When relationships speak to our broken places, they don't allow us to leave those places.

I made a lot of decisions from broken places. My fear of losing companionship and being alone forced me to settle. I was afraid of being with me and didn't truly understand everything that I offered to a companion. When you are in relationships that speak to the broken you; you can't flourish. You will be like a caged bird. You will never be able to explore everything that God has for you when you are in that space. God has the power and ability to set you free from the past and toxic relationships. You must be willing to open your heart and let God move the way He knows best. He is God all by Himself. He knows what you need before you need it.

I received a word of wisdom from my doctor a little while ago. She said her current husband was the love of her life, this was her second marriage and the first ended horribly. She asked, her mother, "How was it possible for one man to treat her well, while the other treated her like crap?" Her mother said, "Never allow any man to change the way you feel about yourself." This statement rang true for me and made me realize how sometimes we as women allow others to influence the feelings, we have about ourselves.

This made me come to terms with painful words spoken against me, while in toxic relationships. I could see how I allowed negative words spoken to me by a significant other, change the way I felt about myself. The saying "sticks and stones may break your bones, but words will never hurt you" wasn't true for me. Bitter words not replaced with the word of God took root and changed the way I saw myself. I allowed people to continuously hurt me and I blamed them for their actions against me without recognizing my own responsibility. I didn't love myself the way I thought I did. My lack of love for myself, showed in the way I allowed others to treat me. Let God change your mindset and show you how wonderful you are. Your worth is not found in the acceptance of man. Your worth is hidden in your Creator. The Bible says, "Before I formed you in your mother's womb, I knew you I set you apart" (Jeremiah 1:5, KJV).

God is calling you to the secret place. He calls you His beloved and wants you to rest at His feet while He pours into you. He wants to tell you how special you are to Him and that you don't need the validation of any man. The culture tells you the fastest way to get over one man is to find another. But the word of God says, it doesn't matter how many men you encounter; they will never be able to quench your thirst. Our Creator desires to commune with us and has placed longings in us that can only be filled by Him. He is the Living Water and we need to run to Him when we feel; lost, depress, lonely, afraid, hurt, and broken.

You don't have to give your body to be valued by a man. You have much more to offer than your curves. There is beauty inside of you and the right man will notice it all. He will want to make a commitment to you in marriage before exploring a deeper level of intimacy with you. Be patient and allow God to reveal the heart of the man He sets before you. Don't trust the butterflies you may be feeling in the moment, it isn't real. Satisfying the flesh is deceptive and destructive; if you aren't careful, you can move too fast and give of yourself without the leading of the Holy Spirit. When we move by emotion and not by the leading of the Holy Spirit, we can find ourselves in some dark places.

The society we live in over sexualizes women and makes sex seem trivial. Don't let people, movies, and music convince you that it's just sex. The enemy of our souls wants us in bondage. He wants us to be slaves to sexual sin and immorality. The devices of Satan are crafty. He makes you believe that God is holding out on you. That's not the case. The enemy always wants to distort our view and make us believe that sex is just about physical pleasure and not the oneness of two souls. God has commanded us to stay away from sexual sin because He knows the pain it will cause long term. When we engage in sexual sin with men that are not our husbands, we develop deadly soul ties. Have you ever wondered why it's so hard for a woman to leave an abusive relationship?

"My people are destroyed for lack of knowledge: because thou hast rejected knowledge, I will also reject thee" (Hosea 4:6, KJV).

When we become aware of what happens in the spiritual realm, when we commit sexual sin; we understand the importance of refraining from it. When a man and a woman have sex, they become one and they are married in the spirit.

"What? Know ye not that he which is joined to an harlot is one body? For two, saith he, shall be one flesh" (1 Corinthians 6:16, KJV).

For this reason, it is so important not to have sex with a man that is not your husband. In marriage, there is a term called consummation. For the marriage to be recognized legally, the husband and wife must have sex. Every man you had sex with that isn't your husband, you have married in the spirit. When God is preparing you for marriage, He must remove all the spiritual connections you have formed with men in the spirit. From the fleshly perspective you may see yourself as single because you don't have a physical husband. But God sees you as married because you have married every man you've had sex with in the spirit. Having sex before marriage opens a host of emotions that you aren't ready to experience. If you focus on abstaining from sex before marriage, you'll be able to make decisions without the leading of the flesh. You'll be able to hear clearly from the Holy Spirit on whether you should proceed with the relationship.

In this process, you'll be given the ability to see the true nature and heart of the man you're dating. Some men don't want relationships, they just want to have sex with you.

"In that day so few men will be left that seven women will fight for each man, saying 'Let us all marry you! We will provide our own food and clothing. Only let us take your name so we won't be mocked as old maids" (Isaiah 4:1, KJV).

The dynamic of the male and female relationship has become perverted. The men of our generation have been emasculated; they have been stripped of their identity and have lost their place as the head of the family. The head of the family is defined as the authority position within the family. There was a time when men equated manhood with being able to protect and provide for their families. In this new culture, Millennials associate manhood with how many women they can sleep with or the amount of money in their bank account. Wickedness has filled the world leaving few healthy eligible bachelors and, as a result, women have settled for the sick ones. The culture has convinced them that loving one woman is a weakness, forgetting that it takes strength to lead the family. Men are supposed to love their wives like Christ loved the church, but times have changed.

"Husbands, love your wives, just as Christ loved the church and gave himself up for her to make her holy, cleansing her by the washing with water through the word" (Ephesians 5:25-26, NIV).

Women have become to independent, not knowing we're supposed to submit ourselves to our own husbands.

"Wives, submit to your husbands as to the Lord" (Ephesians 5:22, NIV).

The enemy always wants to deceive and bring division in marriage. When we're not fully submitted to our husband, we're out of order and can be led astray by the enemy. We must be led by the Holy Spirit to avoid becoming controlling and domineering. A woman that controls and manipulates her husband is not of God, this is a Jezebel spirit. In the bible, in the books of 1st and 2nd Kings, Jezebel was the wife of Ahab, king of Israel. Jezebel promoted the worship of false gods in Israel, harassed and killed God's prophets, and arranged for an innocent man to be falsely charged and executed. She was very wicked in the eyes of the Lord and was later thrown off the balcony and eaten by stray dogs. The culture teaches women to be like Jezebel in the bible, to worship false god's and use manipulation to control men.

"Then Jehu went to Jezreel. When Jezebel heard about it, she painted her eyes, arranged her hair and looked out of a window" (2 King 9:30, NIV).

Jezebel believed she could use her beauty and charm to control Jehu but he knew her heart was wicked and told the servants to throw her down.

"Throw her down! Jehu said. So, they threw her down, and some of her blood spattered the wall and the horses as they trampled her underfoot" (2 Kings 9:33, NIV).

The Lord knows the many habits; we have adopted that come from the kingdom of this world. To prepare for marriage, we must learn submission. God must take us through a process with Him; before we can receive the husband, He has for us. God sets the order of the family and the man is the head.

"For the husband is the head of the wife as Christ is the head of the church, his body, of which he is the Savior" (Ephesians 5:23, KJV).

God never intended for the woman to rule over her husband. When we submit to our husband, we are operating as the body and he is operating as the head. The two become one to accomplish the purposes of God. Both men and women must be prepared by God to function as one in a kingdom marriage. If you can't submit to God; you won't be able to submit to your husband.

"Set me as a seal upon thine heart, as a seal upon thine arm: for love is strong as death; jealousy is cruel as the grave: the coals thereof

are coals of fire, which hath a most vehement flame" (Song of Solomon 8:6, KJV)

Men are projectors and women are receptors, which means men lose strength and the spirit of that man enters the woman. In the Bible, in the book of Judges, there was a man named Samson who had great strength, he fell in love with the wrong woman and it brought about his destruction. "Some time later, he fell in love with a woman in the Valley of Sorek whose name was Delilah" (Judges 16:4, NIV). Samson didn't know that Delilah had been conspiring with his enemy. Several times, Delilah asked Samson to reveal his great strength each time she sent the Philistines to subdue him.

"Then she said to him, "How can you say, 'I love you,' when you won't confide in me? This is the third time you have made a fool of me and haven't told me the secret of your great strength" (Judges 16:15, NIV).

Samson became weak with love; despite his great strength his guard was down and he didn't used discernment. Delilah never had pure intentions for Samson, her motives were wicked and she was only concerned about herself.

"The rulers of the Philistines went to her and said, See if you can lure him into showing you the secret to his great strength and how we can overpower him so we may tie him up and subdue him. Each one of us will give you eleven hundred shekels of silver" (Judges 16:5, NIV).

Samson loved and trusted Delilah and confided in her revealing to her the power of his great strength. "So, he told her everything. No razor has ever been used on my head, he said, because I have been a Nazirite set apart to God since birth. If my head were shaved, my strength would leave me, and I would become as weak as any other man" (Judges 16:17, NIV). Thousands of Philistines failed at their attempt to seize Samson but falling in love with the wrong woman cost him his eyes and life.

"Then the Philistines seized him, gouged out his eyes and took him

down to Gaza. Binding him with bronze shackles, they set him to grinding in the prison" (Judges 16:21, NIV).

Both Adam and Eve were given dominion over the earth by God. The man serves as the covering for the woman and the head of the family, while the woman is the body. The same way in which, we are the body of Christ and Christ is the head.

God had to put Adam to sleep so he could prepare Eve to be a helpmeet. When God is preparing you to be a wife; He must ensure your motives are pure. Women have great power and influence over the men that love them. If our motives aren't in line with the thoughts of God, we can destroy them. We must be led by the Holy Spirit and not by the voice of the enemy.

"You will not surely die, "the serpent said to the woman. For God knows that when you eat of it your eyes will be opened and you will be like God, knowing good and evil" (Genesis 3:4-5, NIV).

The enemy wants to kill steal and destroy the things of God. He hates marriage and if he can't stop it, his desire is to pervert it. The enemy knew the power and influence Eve had over her husband. Therefore, he approaches Eve instead of Adam in the garden of Eden. He knew the only way he could bring about their destruction was going after the one Adam trusted.

"The heart of her husband safely trusts her; So, he will have no lack of gain" (Proverbs 31:11, KJV).

There is more to a relationship than sex. A successful marriage requires intimacy, trust, communication, love, and sacrifice among others things. When God brings a man into your life, He is bringing that man for a purpose. We may not always understand why God is bringing a certain man in our lives. But He has a divine Kingdom purpose for every relationship we encounter. We may be thinking about the moment but God is thinking about future generations and destinies that will be established.

"For my thoughts are not your thoughts, neither are your ways my

ways" (Isaiah 55:8, KJV).

God will never bring someone in your life based solely on attraction, everything He does is for a purpose. He knows everything about your life and what He has called you to do. He knows certain relationships won't help you to cultivate the gifts He has placed inside of you. Even when we make mistakes, God uses everything for His glory. God is doing a new thing in your life. He wants you to let go of the old mindsets that don't bear fruit. He wants to prepare us to be mothers, wives and praying grandmothers to change the trajectory of the culture. If you're a virgin, remain a virgin. If you have decided to practice celibacy, continue that journey. If you're married submit and honor the man God has placed in your life.

∞∞∞

Chapter 8: Wolves

∞ ∞ ∞

"Little Red Riding Hood was enjoying the warm summer day so much, that she didn't notice a dark shadow approaching out of the forest behind her. Suddenly, the wolf appeared beside her. What are you doing out here, little girl? The wolf asked in a voice as friendly as he could muster. I'm on my way to see my Grandma who lives through the forest, near the brook, Little Red Riding Hood replied. Then she realized how late she was and quickly excused herself, rushing down the path to her Grandma's house. The wolf, in the meantime, took a shortcut. The wolf let himself in. Poor Granny did not have time to say another word, before the wolf gobbled her up! The wolf let out a satisfied burp, and then poked through Granny's wardrobe to find a nightgown that he liked. When Little Red Riding Hood entered the little cottage, she could scarcely recognize her Grandmother. But Grandmother! What big ears you have, said Little Red Riding Hood. The better to hear you with, my dear, replied the wolf. But Grandmother! What big eyes you have, said Little Red Riding Hood. The better to see you with, my dear, replied the wolf. But Grandmother! What big teeth you have said Little Red Riding Hood. The better to eat you with, my dear, roared the wolf and he leapt out of the bed and began to chase the little girl... She ran across the room and through the door shouting, Help! Wolf! As loudly as she could."

Wolves are categorized as opportunists; they test their prey, sensing any weakness or vulnerability through visual cues and even through hearing and scent.

In a perfect world, we believe that everyone has good intentions and loves God as we do. But let the truth be told, some people are just good at pretending. Every man doesn't have good intentions for you, some just see you as prey. They may have memorized scripture, they may be the deacon or minister in the church, but their hearts are far from God. They're dangerous! They present themselves as kind hearted, tender, patient and God fearing. But this is an illusion, they have manufactured to gain your trust. Not everyone that enters your life is sent by God. The enemy of our souls will send counterfeits that look the part, to divert you from your destiny. His goal is to keep you in bondage and prevent you from fulfilling your Kingdom purpose.

The first thing the serpent said to Eve was, "Did God really say..." His intentions were to deceive the woman from the beginning of time. Many women are being deceived by men whom are in the church. They're on the outside looking in at the titles and the lies these men tell. God doesn't want His daughters deceived, so, He warns us to make sure to test every spirit. Anyone who has the Holy Spirit won't intentionally deceive you. Men who have a true relationship with God, will have a heart for God and His daughters. He will never pretend to be something he's not.

If he's in ministry his lifestyle must match up with the word of God. The Bible says, you can identify false prophets by the lack of good fruit in their lives. Any man that has a relationship with Jesus will bear good fruit.

"Likewise, every good tree bears good fruit, but a bad tree bears bad fruit" (Matthew 7:17, NIV).

Good fruit and bad fruit can't coexist on the same tree. "Can two walk together except they be agreed" (Amos 3:3, KJV)? Trees that produce good fruit are rooted and have roots, so, they stay planted. But trees that don't produce good fruit will be thrown in the fire and will perish.

Men who have no relationship with the Father can't bear good fruit. Their lives aren't surrendered to God. Therefore, there's no change in their heart. Everything they do is based on religious customs. These individuals haven't been purged by the fire of God.

It's your relationship with Christ that purges you and brings about a heart change.

"If ye keep my commandments, ye shall abide in my love; even as I have kept my Father's commandments, and abide in his love" (John 15:10, KJV).

False prophets can lead the masses astray. It's very important to test every spirit you encounter. You must be vigilant and allow the Holy Spirit to lead you in all truth. A true man of God will never try to convince you to have sex or engage in things of a sinful nature. That's not the fruit of the spirit, which is; love, joy, peace, patience, kindness, goodness, faithfulness, gentleness and self-control.

It's the relationship with the Father that changes an individual, not the scriptures they quote or the title they may carry.

"Watch out for false prophets. They come to you in sheep's clothing, but inwardly they are ferocious wolves" (Matthew 7:15, NIV).

Deception, manipulation and control of any form isn't the fruit of the spirit and comes from the pit of hell. Many believe that only a woman can have a Jezebel spirit but spirits don't have a gender, they have characteristics. A Jezebel spirit seeks to dominate and control. People with this spirit are relentless in their pursuit to gain control of others. They refuse to repent and live a life of idolatry, false teachings and immorality. The enemy uses men with this spirit to keep women bound and from fulfilling their Kingdom purpose.

In the beginning of the relationship, these men pretend to be gentle, patient and understanding. But once they've gain control, they wreak havoc in your life. God never intended for anyone to exert control over another person, this is outside of the Kingdom of God. In fact, He said to be great we must first become servants.

"Jesus called them together and said, You know that those who are regarded as rulers of the Gentiles lord it over them, and their high officials exercise authority over them. Not so with you. Instead,

whoever wants to become great among you must be your servant, and whoever wants to be first must be slave of all. For even the Son of Man did not come to be served, but to serve, and to give his life as a ransom for many" (Mark 10:42-45, NIV).

From the time you're born. You have an enemy whose desire is to kill, steal and destroy you. He studies you and knows your likes and dislikes. In an attempt to deceive you, he'll send someone who looks the part.

"And it came to pass, as we went to prayer, a certain damsel possessed with a spirit of divination met us, which brought her masters much gain by soothsaying: The same followed Paul and us, and cried, saying, These men are the servants of the most high God, Which shew unto us the way of salvation" (Acts 16:16-17 KJV).

Have you ever met the same spirit in a different body? From the outside, they look different, but they're indeed the same spirit wrapped in different flesh. This is a tactic of the enemy to keep you connected to what's familiar. Any relationship that speaks to your past is a trap of the enemy. These individuals are sent as agents of darkness to bring about sabotage, delay and backwardness.

Shortly after rededicating my life to Christ, the enemy began sending several men to get me distracted. The men he would send were charming, handsome, and often spoke candidly about being men of God. But every time I would pray about these individuals the Lord revealed, they weren't who they claimed to be. I had never in the past wholeheartedly given all of my relationships to God. While seeking the Lord, I learned the Lord can see what I cannot see.

"Nothing in all creation is hidden from God's sight. Everything is uncovered and laid bare before the eyes of him to whom we must give account" (Hebrews 4:13, NIV).

I now understood the importance of submitting every relationship before the Lord. As women of God, we need relationships that are ordained by God. That will push us closer to God.

It was Mother's Day weekend. My cousin, aunt, mom and I all decided to go to Atlantic City for a concert. The next day we went to a restaurant to get some breakfast before hitting the road. As we were chatting, enjoying our breakfast, I noticed this guy staring at me. I thought nothing of it at first and continued to eat my breakfast. A few moments later, I got up to use the restroom. When I came out the same guy was waiting for me outside of the restroom. I was startled at first but he quickly introduced himself. He said, he didn't want to bother me while I was with my family. But he thought I was beautiful and had to say hello. He asked, if I was single and I said yes, we then preceded to exchange numbers. Although, we both lived in different states, we figured our friendship could develop long distance.

A few weeks into our conversation, I learned, he taught sixth grade, had no children and came from a small family. He was charming, handsome, smart and claimed to be a follower of Christ. We both loved children and both spoke of being married in the future. I couldn't help but wonder if this was the man God had for me.

As the weeks progressed and the conversations increased. I begin to pray asking God to reveal his true intentions. My prayer at the time was, "God please give me sight beyond what I can see." This was my prayer every day all the way up to our first date. For our first date, we decided that it would be a good idea for him to come to my city, go to church and get lunch after. The night before our scheduled first date, I received a phone call from him. He decided, to come earlier than expected.

A few hours later, I woke up to a voicemail at 3am. He stated, he was at the train station and needed to be picked up. He didn't realize, the train didn't run that early in the morning.

I thought this was weird, considering, we agreed to meet Sunday morning at 9am. I must admit, several red flags went up! I played it cool. And let him know, I was unable to pick him up so early in the morning. He was a little upset initially but apologized for coming early and blamed it on the excitement of our first date. He called again, and said, he brought a change of clothes and needed somewhere to change. I let him know, I was uncomfortable with him knowing where I lived.

His actions at this point were speaking much louder than his previous words. Before, I laid back down to rest. I prayed and ask God to reveal Him to me in a way I couldn't ignore. Shortly after falling back to sleep, I woke up terrified from a dream of him trying to harm me. I began to pray again and heard the Lord telling me that this guy was not sent by Him.

I knew at that moment; he was a wolf in sheep's clothing. Pretending, he was someone else to gain my trust. The Lord showed me, this guy was sent by the enemy.

I'm so thankful, I prayed and asked God to reveal his true intentions. I'm not sure what would've happened if I continued to date him. I ended things and moved on. From the outside looking in, he seemed like the perfect gentleman. But the Lord revealed, he had motives from the beginning. Motives that could only be revealed by the Holy Spirit.

It's very important to invite God into every relationship we entertain. Regardless of how perfect the guy may seem. God can show you things that reside deep within his heart. When we let our Creator be Lord over our lives, He can reveal the true nature of a man. We don't have the power to know the true heart of a man until it's revealed by their actions. God knows the true heart of a person before any actions are revealed.

"He said, May God deal with me, be it ever so severely, if the head of Elisha son of Shaphat remains on his shoulders today! Now Elisha was sitting in his house, and the elders were sitting with him. The king sent a messenger ahead, but before he arrived, Elisha said to the elders,

"Don't you see how this murderer is sending someone to cut off my head? Look, when the messenger comes, shut the door and hold it shut against him. Is not the sound of his master's footsteps behind him" (2 Kings 6:31-32, NIV)?

God allowed Elisha to see the true intentions of the king. He sent a messenger to deceive Elisha. He wanted him to think he was coming in peace, but he was behind the messenger. His true desire was to cut Elisha's head off. If Elisha wasn't in tune with the Holy Spirit, he could've died. Not knowing the king sought his life. Our heavenly Father wants to give us that same discernment and give us spiritual insight in all relationships. These things can only be revealed by the spiritual eyes and requires a relationship with the Almighty God.

In order to navigate these relationships, you must use spiritual discernment to test every spirit. Spiritual discernment requires you to submit the relationship to God. You do this by praying and asking the Lord to give you sight beyond what you can see. When you do this, God will give you the spiritual discernment needed to see beyond the words and actions of a person. The Lord showed me the importance of submitting every relationship before Him. It doesn't matter how nice a man may seem, submit the relationship to the Lord and allow the Holy Spirit to lead you in every decision.

Being in tune with the spirit of the Lord is crucial when dating. The enemy uses our weaknesses against us and will introduce relationships that feed our need for instant gratification. Relationships that are sent by God will edify and push you toward your purpose. Relationships that are sent by Satan will derail your destiny and push you further away from God. These relationships don't feed your spirit but encourage the sinful way of life, you were delivered from.

"Be sober, be watchful: your adversary the devil, as a roaring lion, walketh about, seeking whom he may devour" (1 Peter 5:8, KJV).

His goal is to destroy your life by keeping you distracted from the things that God is calling you to do. He does this by sending you a counterfeit. Someone who seems to be exactly what you want on the outside but on the inside, they are raging wolves. The devil doesn't always appear with horns and a pitch fork, sometimes he reveals himself as a new relationship. If you're not careful and fully submitted to God. You can be misled by the enemy. The Lord communicates His thoughts in many ways depending on the individual.

Many times, we ignore the red flags we perceive in relationships. Sometimes it's that uneasy feeling in your spirit or nudging from family and friends. It may be certain things in his actions that don't sit right with you, or the way he treats his mother. Whichever way, the Lord is communicating that something isn't right. Please take heed! God will always send warnings before the situation turns for the worst. When we ignore the Holy Spirit, we can find ourselves in some dangerous places.

I've always heard stories of how the perfect man turned into the devil and often wondered how that could be possible. The Lord showed me that these women looked at the outward appearance and didn't realize they were dealing with a wolf in sheep's clothing. They were deceived by these men, believing that they were sent by God. But they were sent by the enemy to destroy them. God wants the best for His daughters. He wants us entering healthy relationships that will help us thrive and get closer to Him. God will never send you a man that will pull you away from Him. The enemy will use relationships to distract you from your purpose and keep you bound. His goal is to get you to form unhealthy bonds with men, who aren't for you. The relationships that aren't God ordained will seem too good to be true.

The wolf will often have the words of a sheep to gain your trust and deceive you. Their desires are lustful and they only want to defile you. They will prey on your weaknesses and vulnerabilities, so they can satisfy their lustful desires. The man God has for you will cover you and give you his last name.

In the Bible, there was a man named Ammon who was infatuated with Tamar his half-sister. "And Amnon was so vexed, that he fell sick for 'his sister Tamar; for she was a virgin; and Amnon thought it hard for him to do anything to her" (2 Samuel 13:2, KJV). Amnon pretended to be sick, so, Tamar could take care of him. When he had her close enough to him, he raped her. She begged him not to, but instead, suggested, he ask her father the King for her hand in marriage. He refused. After he defiled her body, he told her to leave.

"Then Amnon hated her exceedingly; so that the hatred wherewith he hated her was greater than the love wherewith he had loved her. And Amnon said unto her, Arise, be gone" (2 Samuel 13:15, KJV).

Amnon never loved Tamar, the bible says that love is patient, kind and isn't self-seeking or self-serving. His desire for her was always lustful in nature. He sought to defile her. In biblical times, if a man raped a woman, it was customary for him to marry her due to the violation.

"If a man happens to meet a virgin who is not pledged to be married and rapes her and they are discovered, he shall pay the girl's father fifty shekels of silver. He must marry the girl, for he has violated her" (Deuteronomy 22:28-29, NIV).

Although, we're not in biblical times and this is considered incest. The lesson here remains the same. There are men who come into your life who don't want to marry you. They only want to use you for their own selfish gain.

God loves His daughters and doesn't want us to fall victim to the tactics of the enemy. Tamar was deceived by her half-brother. There are men, that don't have good intentions for you. They'll lie to fulfill the passions of their own lust. Our heavenly Father doesn't want to see us hurt by men that don't respect and appreciate us. He doesn't want us taken advantage of by sick men, who only want to fulfill their lustful desires. God doesn't want us making choices based on what the guy appears to be.

When you have standards a lot of men will walk away. But trust me, the right man will stay and be there for the long haul. The bald eagle can fly up to 10,000 feet in the air and can see another eagle up to 50 miles away. Bring your standards up to that of the bald eagle, and allow God to reveal your mate while in purpose. Don't lower your standards to fit the needs of a man, make him come up to your standards. If he can't come up to your standards, fly alone until the right man comes. Wait on the Lord.

"But they that wait upon the Lord shall renew their strength; they shall mount up with wings as eagles; they shall run, and not be weary; and they shall walk, and not faint" (Isaiah 40:31, KJV).

Don't give the gift God has given you for your husband. To a man who won't be in your life five or ten years down the road. A man that really loves you and sees the God in you. Will want to make a life-long commitment to you in marriage. Don't conform to the standards of the culture. Allow God to show you what he has prepared for you before the foundations of the earth was formed. The culture shows you all the highlights but never exposes the ugly truths.

∞ ∞ ∞

Chapter 9: When God Says No!

∞ ∞ ∞

I'm sure we all can agree, there were times in our lives; when we deliberately disobeyed our parents. At the time, we thought, we knew better than them. The lessons we learned along the way served as a reminder to the words we too often forget. My father and mother taught me many lessons while growing up and one of those was to never gamble. I can still hear my father's voice saying, "Dee, you'll never get something for nothing." He would say things like, "You may think you're getting over in the moment but you're only fooling yourself." I'll never forget being a naive eighteen-year-old believing that I would get something for nothing. One afternoon, I went to the Sprint store to get my phone serviced. I remember seeing three older men and a woman outside the store playing a game of three-card Monte. As I was leaving, I overheard the lady say, 'If I had twenty dollars, I could join the game and possibly win eighty dollars.'

The lust of the flesh took over and before I knew it. I was playing one-card molly. I won the first eighty dollars but didn't stop there. I had to continue. Twenty-five minutes later I lost over five-hundred dollars. I don't even know how it happened. All I know is I felt numb. My heart sink to the bottom of my stomach. My father's words echoed in my head, "Dee you'll never get something for nothing." The words my father spoke so long ago finally resonated. In a matter of minutes, I had gambled away a week's paycheck with the hopes of initially winning eighty dollars. My father's words always came back at the most opportune times. On this day, I learned a valuable lesson about sowing and reaping, as well as, honoring your mother and father.

"When I was a child, I spake as a child, I understood as a child, I thought as a child: but when I became a man, I put away childish

things" (1 Corinthians 13:11, KJV).

When our parents tell us "no" it's not to harm us, but to protect us from dangers we may not be aware of. It was something about hearing the word "no" that would instantly make me unhappy. Now that I'm a mother, I find myself telling my daughter no often. I realize now that all the "no's" I heard as a child was my parents' way of protecting me from things, I was too young to understand. Scripture teaches us that the Lord loves us so much that He will not withhold any good thing. When our heavenly Father tells us "no," He is telling us for a reason.

The Lord sees and knows all. He wrote the end before He wrote the beginning. He knows every event that will occur in your life. He knows the relationship you're about to enter isn't a good one. He knows the friend you grew up with is secretly jealous of you. He knows the opportunities that seem good; will ultimately end in disaster. The Lord's desire is always to protect you and keep you in alignment with His plans and purpose for your life.

Every opportunity you encounter isn't always from God nor is it His best for you. Many times, the enemy of our souls will copycat the things of God to produce a counterfeit blessing to take us off the path of righteousness. The Lord wants you to know how cunning your enemy is and will allow you to stumble if you don't hearken to His voice and warnings. In this way, you gain wisdom and strength to push toward the battle ahead.

"The fear of God is the beginning of wisdom" (Proverbs 9:10, KJV).

When you have a healthy fear of the Lord, your life is governed differently. You aren't concerned with the opinions of people only the purpose and plans God has for your life. When we're in direct alignment with the Father, He can show us the coming danger as well as any pitfalls the enemy is placing in our lives. God loves us so much and will always send warnings before destruction. When we're obedient to His word, we can reap the benefits of the promise.

"For the Lord disciplines the one He loves, and He chastises every son whom He receives" (Hebrews 12:6, KJV).

When we're disobedient to the word of the Lord, we must deal with the outcome of our actions. "You may not be able to hear but you can feel," is a phrase my old neighbor would often say. This woman was full of wisdom and would speak with me often about the many lessons the Lord taught her. God will allow trials and tribulation to teach you valuable lessons for the journey ahead. There are times we'll learn our lessons through word of knowledge and other times God must take us through a refining process.

"But he knoweth the way that I take: when he hath tried me, I shall come forth as gold" (Job 23:10, KJV).

These tests are designed to increase your faith and purify your motivations. There are times in life when God will let us hit rock bottom to teach us the lessons from the low place. During these times, our heavenly Father is using trials to strengthen us. God wants us to operate out of truth. He will provide us with the steps we need to take, to stay connected to Him. It's our job to stay connected to the source and heed the warnings.

Everyone who starts with you, aren't meant to finish with you. When God says "no," you must be obedient, if you want to inherit the promise. God is always doing a new thing even when we don't perceive it. Our focus may be on yesterday but God's focus is always on the future. "Behold, I will do a new thing; now it shall spring forth; shall ye not know it? I will even make a way in the wilderness, and rivers in the desert" (Isaiah 43:19, KJV). God must remove the old and the familiar to bring the new. If God doesn't allow a person to continue with you, it's because they aren't apart of His divine destiny for your life. He must divinely orchestrate every relationship in your life, so you can reach His expected end.

At one point, the Lord told me that a romantic relationship with a certain person would forfeit my destiny. At the time, I was heartbroken not understanding God's thoughts and ways. This person had played a major role in my life. I never imagined, the closer I got with God the more the relationship with that person would drift away. The Lord began to reveal more things about the relationship, showing me, it no longer served a purpose in my life. At which point, I was told by God to let it go. This was hard for me because I had developed my own attachments. The Lord showed me that nothing and no one comes before His purposes and plans. There's no in the middle, you're either for Him or against Him.

"Now when Joshua was near Jericho, he looked up and saw a man standing in front of him with a drawn sword in his hand. Joshua went up to him and asked, Are you for us or for our enemies? Neither, he replied, but as commander of the army of the Lord I have now come. Then Joshua fell facedown to the ground in reverence, and asked him, What message does my Lord have for his servant" (Joshua 5:13-14, NIV)?

When you walk in the will of God. You must be prepared to draw a line in the sand against anyone or anything that stands in the way of you getting to your destiny. You can't be afraid to walk away from people or things that no longer serve a purpose. You must be fully submitted to the plans and purposes of God. When He says "no", you must hearken to His voice.

If you take a moment and reflect on all the relationships the Lord removed from your life. You'll see they no longer served a purpose. If we don't allow God to remove the old. We'll never be able to accommodate the new. Everything God does is purposeful. He'll never place a relationship in your life that serves no purpose.

When God brings a man into your life. It won't be based on anything fleshly, but will be spiritual in nature. You'll know he's your husband not by flesh, but by the revelation from the Holy Spirit in the secret place. You may not always understand the ways or thoughts of God. But your job as the sheep is to follow the Good Shepherd.

"For my thoughts are not your thoughts, neither are your ways my ways, saith the Lord" (Isaiah 55:8, KJV).

God doesn't need our approval to move. He requires our obedience. The Lord wants us to walk by faith and not by sight, so, He won't reveal the complete plan. It's your job to trust and move, when He says move. God doesn't require anything from us but our obedience and a willing heart. When you love God, you want to obey and keep His commandments. When God calls you, He is calling you to partner with Him to do something mighty in the world. The things of God require a different level of obedience and sacrifice. It requires tunnel vision and a mindset that is fully submitted to God's will and way.

God must introduce you to a different level of discipline, so, you're able to manage all that He is giving you. There are habits that you have developed over time that need to be abandoned, as well as behaviors that need to change.

God will never give you something you haven't prepared for. When much is given, much is required. Our heavenly Father doesn't operate in confusion and will never provide you with more than you can manage. You may be asking God for a husband, financial prosperity, a new home, or for your business or ministry to grow. But if you haven't taken the practical steps that are within your control. How can you expect your heavenly Father to move supernaturally? Everything you do with God is a partnership and requires your skin in the game. Sometimes God says "no" to your request, because, He knows the blessing will destroy you.

He told them, " The harvest is plentiful, but the workers are few. Ask the Lord of the harvest, therefore, to send out workers into his harvest field" (Luke 10:2, NLT).

The blessing's already ready! But you must be willing to roll up your sleeves and partner with your heavenly Father to be able to reap the harvest. God's timing is perfect. He never sleeps nor slumbers, so whatever He has for us will always be on time.

Ecclesiastes 3:1 says "to everything there is a season, and a time to every purpose under the heaven." God's always focused on His plans and purposes for our lives.

When we're directly aligned with the will and way of our heavenly Father. Every relationship and opportunity will be used to produce fruit in every season. God created you in his image. He knows the right amount of pressure required to produce good fruit in your life. When God says "no," He is positioning you for His promises.

The good times don't always show the blessings and prosperity. It's in those dark places, when God puts the fire back into our bellies, whispers in our ear and tells us how special and wonderfully made we are. God speaks to you in those dry places and strengthens your faith.

When God takes you through His purging fire. He's preparing you for the work ahead. In those moments, He's stripping you of everything that's not like Him and giving you a new identity. It's in the consuming fire of God that we learn exactly who the Almighty has called us to be. Many times, we find ourselves in the prison just like Paul and Silas not knowing that the prison will prepare us for our next assignment. God's using those moments when we're imprisoned, to stretch us in places we have yet to be stretched. His great refining process prepares us for the moments we have yet to encounter.

God knows the areas in your life that need pruning. When we surrender our lives to God. We're telling the Potter to mold us into the women, He wants us to be. Everything that happens in our lives is divinely orchestrated by the Father. He has a plan and a purpose for all the pain we've endured.

The love of God exposes dry areas, so, we can heal and become better versions of ourselves. When the spirit of the Lord leads you to dark desolate places in your mind. He's revealing the areas in your life that need to be surrendered. God's a gentleman. He'll reveal the areas that need to be surrendered but it is our job to open our hearts. God doesn't allow anything that happened to us to be done in vain. He uses everything we've been through for His glory. You may not understand the process but know God's in control of your destiny.

"And we know that all things work together for good to them that love God, to them who are the called according to his purpose" (Romans 8:28, KJV).

When every area of our lives is submitted to God, we have freedom. We're no longer bound by the things of the world and or the past. In this place, God can move mountains and open the doors, no man can shut and close the doors, no man can open.

"These things saith He that is holy, He that is true, He that hath the key of David, He that openeth and no man shutteth, and shutteth and no man openeth" (Revelation 3:7, KJV).

Delay doesn't always mean denial. Sometimes, we must deny instant gratification, to allow our heavenly Father to do the work needed behind the scenes. In most cases, this will catapult us into our divine destiny.

God never removes relationships or opportunities to punish us. When the Lord says "no" to certain relationships, friendships or opportunities, He's subtracting what you don't need. To make room for what you will need in the future. God will never remove anything good without replacing it with something better. When God says "no" to the good thing, know that He has something better waiting for you.

Our God is purposeful, so, every relationship and opportunity must serve a purpose in our lives. Anything that doesn't serve a purpose in your life can be used by the enemy to distract you from the things that you're called to. We're all placed on Earth for the purposes of God. There's nothing more important than fulfilling the destiny God has placed on your life. Don't allow anyone to keep you in a place, where you can't grow and develop in the things of

God. Every relationship in your life must serve a purpose and if it doesn't serve a purpose, you must ask yourself is this relationship ordained by God. Even the relationship between Jesus and Judas served its purpose by bringing Jesus closer to the cross.

You must be willing to let go of the familiar and step into uncharted territory. Jesus said in John 16:33, "Take heart I have overcome the world." The window of opportunity is open. Everything holding you back from your destiny was crucified on the cross. God needs your complete devotion and belief in who He is, so, you can step into the fullness of your destiny.

Our life is not our own, we're all connected for a greater purpose. When God begins to show you the true colors of the closest people to you, believe Him. There are some relationships we're comfortable with that don't produce good fruit in our lives. There are other relationships that need to be cultivated for our growth.

If you aren't careful, you can find yourself idolizing people, money, ministry, and/or success. As God begins to bring you closer to Him, He will test your obedience and love for Him by telling you to remove things and people in your life that are closest to you. The word of God declares,

"Thou shalt have no other Gods before me" (Exodus 20:3, KJV).

Anything we put before God is an idol. At times, we vent to our friends and or family about issues that are beyond their control. It's a form of idolatry to put people before God. Our heavenly Father wants us to come to His throne of grace with every issue we have. He's your listening ear and the only One that has the power to deliver you. He wants to mend your broken heart and restore everything you've lost. When God says "no"! It isn't to punish you, but to push you closer to your destiny!

∞ ∞ ∞

∞ ∞ ∞

"Favor is deceitful, and beauty is vain: but a woman that feareth the Lord, she shall be praised" (Proverbs 31:30, KJV).

As we grow older and wiser, we realize, the physical attributes of our bodies will change. Our once perky breasts will begin to sag, our facial features may become more defined. Our hips will begin to spread and we may pick up an extra five or ten pounds. The world we live in today determines one's value based on material possessions or outward beauty. Beauty is temporary and will fade; there will always be someone more beautiful or younger looking. Wealth is meaningless as well. You can have all the money in the world but be tormented in your mind and won't be able to enjoy the fruits of your labor. Your career can't make you happy or bring you closer to God. God cares nothing about your great wealth, influence or beauty. It's impossible to bribe God.

"For the LORD your God is God of gods and Lord of lords, the great God, mighty and awesome, who shows no partiality and accepts no bribes" (Deuteronomy 10:17, NIV).

Our Creator doesn't look at outward beauty or the works of your hands, or see you the way the world sees you. The only thing that matters to Him is your heart posture.

"But the Lord said unto Samuel, Look not on his countenance, or on the height of his stature because I have refused him; for the Lord seeth not as man seethe; for man looketh on the outward appearance, but the Lord looketh on the heart" (1 Samuel 16:7, KJV).

The Lord searches every heart and knows your true motives. You may be able to fool people but you can't fool God. He sees the real you, not the person you pretend to be. He knows your insecurities, doubts, failures and why you, do the things you do. His desire is to purify your heart, so your confidence can be established in Him and not in yourself, wealth or the praise of people.

"There will be terrible times in the last days. People will be lovers of themselves, lovers of money, boastful, proud, abusive, disobedient to their parents, ungrateful, unholy, without love, unforgiving, slanderous, without self-control, brutal, not lovers of the good, treacherous, rash, conceited, lovers of pleasure rather than lovers of God having a form of godliness but denying its power. Have nothing to do with them" (2 Timothy 3:1-5, NIV).

The times have changed and people have become lovers of themselves. They're boastful, prideful and full of greed. Everything they do is for selfish ambition and the admiration of people. Being arrogant, rude and brutal to one another is celebrated in our society. If you don't agree turn on the News/CNN or pick up your local newspaper any day of the week. Humans have waged war on themselves! No one dares to step outside of their own bubble to help someone else. We're living in perilous times....

Being beautiful and successful is considered the Holy Grail today; but none of our blood has filled this cup. We're not God and shouldn't illicit praise from people. Everything we have has been given to us. When we forget this, we lose sight of others and our purpose for being on earth.

Vanity is recognizing only the accomplishments or appearance of oneself without the humility to appreciate the merit of others, including God. Narcissism is defined as the pursuit of gratification from vanity or egotistic admiration of one's idealized self-image and attributes. It's a personality disorder that forces people to promote themselves, so others can give them praise. The term narcissism comes from Greek Mythology in which a young man named Narcissus fell in love with his own reflection.

Humans aren't the first ones to inhibit this spirit; the first narcissist was Satan himself. Satan was so beautiful and the master musician. Because of his great beauty and talent. He began to have a false sense of his identity; not recognizing he was the creation not the creator. The creation can never fully comprehend the Creator. The fall of Satan and ⅓ of the angels in heaven was due to pride. When you're prideful, you refuse to submit yourself to the Almighty assuming you're like God or can compare yourself to God. "Pride goeth before the fall and a haughty spirit before destruction" (Proverbs 16:18, KJV). Satan began promoting himself thinking he was like the most high.

"I will ascend above the heights of the clouds; I will be like the Most High" (Isaiah 14:14, KJV).

Satan was casted out of heaven because the Lord found iniquity in his heart. "Thou wast perfect in thy ways from the day that thou wast created, till iniquity was found in thee. By the multitude of thy merchandise, they have filled the midst of thee with violence, and thou hast sinned: therefore, I will cast thee as profane out of the mountain of God: and I will destroy thee, O covering cherub, from the midst of the stones of fire" (Ezekiel 28:15-16, KJV). Anytime you take pride in yourself or the work of your own hands without acknowledging God you're operating out of pride. We must always give the glory and honor to the Lord because He's the Creator of everything. We didn't create ourselves; we can't wake ourselves up in the morning. Everything we have and will accomplish is a gift from God. "The earth is the Lord's, and the fullness thereof; the world, and they that dwell therein" (Psalm 24:1, KJV).

"In the same way, be submissive to those who are older. All of you, clothe yourselves with humility toward one another, because, God opposes the proud but gives grace to the humble. Humble, yourselves, therefore, under God's mighty hand, that he may lift you up in due time" (1 Peter 5:5-6, NIV).

Pride says, praise me because I have created everything with my own hands. Humility says, everything I have belongs to God and all the blessings are the favor of God sprinkled over my life. Pride is the opposite of humility; it causes people to covet the flattery of others. Proposing every action for the acknowledgement and praise of people. When you seek to please people and not God; you're in a dangerous place. You'll be blown by the winds of the world. You won't be rooted in truth; you'll be rooted in the opinions of others. When they applaud you, you'll be ecstatic. When they relinquish their praise, you will fall apart. When you seek the validation from others, people can control your thoughts and actions. You should never seek the praise or admiration of people, everything you do should be to please your heavenly Father.

"For the Lord will be your confidence and will keep your foot from being snared" (Proverbs 3:26, NIV).

Our heavenly Father doesn't mind us being confident. He just wants us to have confidence in who He has called us to be, not in ourselves, or the work of our hands. He wants us to know that our identity is not in the things of this world or our talents, beauty or abilities, but is found in Christ.

People who are vain, find their confidence in their beauty, the affirmation of people and things they possess. These individuals are hurting. They use temporary things and people to give them the validation, they so desperately need. They associate their value with things that are meaningless. When they're stripped of these things. They don't know or understand their place in society.

Everything external is temporary, when you died you can't take any of it with you. The earth and the fullness thereof belong to God, the authority or power you have on earth means nothing to God. None of us have the power to add one minute to our lives.

"Who of you by worrying can add a single hour to his life? Since you cannot do this very little thing, why do you worry about the rest" (Luke 12:25-26, NIV)?

We shouldn't be concerned with what people think or how

they feel about us. I know this is easier said than done. It takes us constantly sitting at the feet of Jesus getting the affirmation that many of us never received as children. Many people that suffer from narcissistic behavior were rejected as children. People who have been rejected often find ways to protect themselves by developing a false sense of identity. This allows them to conceal the internal hurt they feel. They seek admiration and or affluence to feel better about themselves and find value in their life.

Narcissism is dangerous because it creates an open door in your life. Satan monitors you throughout your life. He looks for open doors, so, he can operate freely without your knowledge. He uses the things that hurt you in your past, so he can form bondages that follow you into adulthood and wreak havoc in your life.

"By thy great wisdom and by thy traffick hast thou increased thy riches, and thine heart is lifted up because of thy riches" (Ezekiel 28:5, KJV).

Narcissism comes from the pit of hell and is a notion that was originated by Satan. Satan uses narcissism to make people place value in things that are meaningless. When we begin to put value in the things that are meaningless, we begin to lose sight of the things that really matter. Our motives become impure and we operate out of the wrong spirit. God doesn't mind you having riches or beauty; it was never his desire for you to live in poverty or lack. But when you begin to associate your worth with the things of this world, you're in error. You aren't operating out of the right spirit. These things can bring destruction in your life. When God gives gifts and or great wisdom to obtain wealth, we must remain humble and know that it wasn't us but the Almighty. You must stay in the presence of God, so He can purify you, to keep you from sin. If you don't, you can begin to create idols out of the wisdom and the riches you've obtained.

"Praise the Lord, O my soul: all my inmost being, praise his holy name" (Psalm 103:1, NIV).

The enemy is always trying to steal your praise because he hates the admiration of God. When we praise God in the good and bad times. It confuses the enemy. The enemy will attempt to set the stage to make everything seem like it's not working out. He wants to put you in a defeated state of mind and convince you to give up on your purpose. He wants you to deny God's power and authority in your life. Therefore, God tells us that we must walk by faith and not by sight. If we walk by sight, we're believing the illusions the enemy has placed in front of us.

Satan is not a creator and therefore everything that he does is counterfeit and made to deceive God's people. He's not able to create something original, he imitates and perverts what God has already created. He will always present an illusion of the promise to get you to worship himself and not the true and living God. Satan doesn't change the way he operates. The same tactics he used to tempt Jesus in the garden of Gethsemane are the same one's used today. He tried to tempt Jesus with the pride of life. He didn't want Jesus to continue in His purpose and be the Savior for all of humanity.

"And the devil, taking him up into a high mountain, shewed unto him all the kingdoms of the world in a moment of time. And the devil said unto him, all this power will I give thee, and the glory of them: for that is delivered unto me; and to whomsoever I will I give it. If thou therefore wilt worship me, all shall be thine. And Jesus answered and said unto him, get thee behind me, Satan: for it is written, thou shalt worship the Lord thy God, and him only shalt thou serve" (Luke 4:5-8, KJV).

Satan wanted Jesus to bow down to him and worship the idols he placed in front of Him. Satan is very crafty; he'll always mix truth with a lie to get you to believe what he presents is just as real as the promises of God. He'll use the things you desire most to become a snare to you. The word of God tells us, "Do not be anxious about anything, but in every situation, by prayer and petition, with thanksgiving, present your requests to God. And the peace of God, which transcends all understanding, will guard your hearts and your minds in Christ Jesus" (Philippians 4:6-7, NIV). Satan wants you to become impatient with the things of God. So, you're willing to accept a counterfeit blessing and abort your purpose. Satan will always make sin look good. He knows the things of God produce life and the things he presents are death.

"For the wages of sin is death; but the gift of God is eternal life through Jesus Christ our Lord" (Romans 6:23, KJV).

Satan's goal is to kill, steal, and destroy the people of God. He knows, if he can steal your praise. He can take away your faith in the Almighty God and put it in yourself or worthless idols. He wants you to have your faith in things that are temporary and that have no power. When you worship beauty, money, clothes, cars, titles, careers, gifts and other worldly possessions. They become your God. You have replaced the true and living God with temporary pleasures that can't save you.

Praise was never orchestrated for God; it was given to man as a gift to keep him in relationship with the Father. "The God who made the world and everything in it is the Lord of heaven and earth and does not live in temples built by hands. And he is not served by human hands, as if he needed anything, because he himself gives all men life and breath and everything else" (Acts 17:24-25, NIV). God is self-sufficient, He doesn't need our praise. When we praise God, we're submitting ourselves to the Father and keeping ourselves from falling victim to pride. "Submit yourselves therefore to God. Resist the devil, and he will flee from you" (James 4:7, KJV).

"Bel boweth down, Nebo stoopeth, their idols were upon the beasts, and upon the cattle: your carriages were heavy laden; they are a burden to the weary beast. They stoop, they bow down together; they could not deliver the burden, but themselves are gone into captivity" (Isaiah 46:1-2, KJV).

The Israelites begin to worship the idols of the foreign land they were in and when the enemy attacked them, the idols they created couldn't keep them from going into captivity. When you begin to worship these things or the work of your hands, you take the glory from God and become like Satan. Satan had a false sense of identity and believed he was like God. When you worship anything other than the true and living God, you're practicing idolatry. Satan knows, when we put our trust in the things of this world, we have no power. He wants to take your power and wants you to be like him seeking the admiration from people for the things you have. He doesn't want God to get the glory; he wants you to place your trust in things that are meaningless. He was cast out of heaven because he was full of pride and refused to give God the glory.

"How art thou fallen from heaven, O Lucifer, son of the morning! How art thou cut down to the ground, which didst weaken the nations" (Isaiah 14:12, KJV)!

Satan uses the pride of life to tempt people into believing that their accomplishments and the temporary things of this world should grant them admiration from people. They refuse to acknowledge the true and living God. The riches and wealth they have accumulated have been used as a snare by the enemy. The enemy wants you to compare yourself to these individuals, so, you can become envious and desire what they have and setup idols in your heart.

I remember I found myself being envious of those people. Asking God, why I had to work so hard; while I felt others had been given a free pass. I couldn't understand why so many people with great faith had experienced some of the worst conditions. From the outside looking in others seemed to be thriving. I'll never forget the Lord telling me to read Psalm 73. In this chapter, the writer talks about how he saw the wicked prosper and how he almost slipped into the snare of the enemy. He started believing, the good he did was worthless because he hadn't seen the immediate prosperity. "Verily I have cleansed my heart in vain, and washed my hands in innocency" (Psalm 73:13, KJV). He saw how the wicked prospered despite their pride and greed.

"Therefore, pride compasseth them about as a chain; violence covereth them as a garment. Their eyes stand out with fatness: they have more than heart could wish" (Psalm 73:6-7, KJV).

These people had become so prideful because of the wealth they acquired that they blasphemed God and spoke loftily against the oppressed. There are people in the world who belive they are 'gods' because of their great wealth or talents. But the Lord says, they're on a path to destruction. Their accumulation of wealth cannot keep them from the grave or an eternity in Hell. Although on the outside looking in, these people seemed to prosper, but their end would be destruction. The Lord showed me that the idols they setup had become their God. The pride of life had blinded them and they believed they were in control of their own destinies.

"Surely, thou didst set them in slippery places: thou castedst them down into destruction" (Psalm 73:18, KJV).

The Lord is always searching for someone who is after His own heart. "For those who exalt themselves will be humbled, and those who humble themselves will be exalted" (Luke 14:11, KJV).

On the other hand; many people believe they're humble because they don't drive an expensive car, have wealth, wear expensive clothing or live in a big house. But the true nature of humility has nothing to do with your financial status, what you wear, how big your house is or the car you drive. Some of the wealthiest people are humble and some of the poorest poor are vain and full of pride. God doesn't see people the way man sees people. He doesn't say, "hey she's driving a BMW or lives in a mansion, so, she's not humble." He's always looking at your secret motivations.

We must do a heart check, to make sure we're in direct alignment with the Father. Ask yourself! Did you choose the car because you want people to praise you? Does driving this car change the way you treat people? Does your wealth and status make you believe that you're like God? Better than other people and or in control of your destiny? Do you believe that the beauty you possess is the work of your hands or use your beauty to manipulate men? Do you seek the adoration from people because of the things you possess? God's always testing us to make sure the desires of our hearts are pure. If you desire these things, so people can praise you and not the true and living God, then the desires of your heart are wicked. God is forgiving and merciful and wants us to come to him so He can purify us.

"Keep thy heart with all diligence; for out of it are the issues of life" (Proverbs 4:23, KJV).

The Lord is only concerned with the motives behind your works. You can accomplish many great things in your life. But if your motives are wrong, then it is all meaningless to God.

"Take heed that ye do not your alms before men, to be seen of them: otherwise ye have no reward of your Father which is in Heaven" (Matthew 6:1, KJV).

Everything we do must be done in love. When Jesus died for our sins, it was out of love. Our motives for everything we do, must be pure. If they aren't pure, we're doing them in vain. The Lord won't honor them. If your motivations aren't because you love people and want to do the will of the Father. You must ask the Lord to clean your heart. Ask the Lord to give you the confidence to know who you are in Him. So, everything you do flows from your love for Him and not the adoration of people.

When we begin to do this, God can clean our hearts and our motives. When we come to God with our broken pieces, He can begin to put us back together. He doesn't punish you based on things from your past or your wrong way of thinking. He knows where every thought originated. He wants you to be confident in who He is and have the right motivations.

When God begins to give us the confidence that we have lacked growing up. We will see that our motives for everything will begin to change. When we make decisions, they will be from the right place. There will be peaks and valleys in your life, but the thing to stay focused on is your Creator. When your focus is on your Creator and not on the things of this world, you have built a solid foundation; one that will last. If your foundation is built on temporary things that are meaningless. When the wind blows, your house will fall apart.

∞ ∞ ∞

∞ ∞ ∞

"For the creation waits in eager expectation for the children of God to be revealed" (Romans 8:19, NIV).

As a child, I remember vividly singing this song by the Mississippi Children's Choir called, "There is Hope" the lyrics recite:

"People are dying everywhere, drugs are taking them away,
Children are crying all around, a solution must be found."
"Gangs are destroying all our schools, no more interest in the golden rule; they took prayer out of the class, tell me how long will it last?"
"Yes, there is hope, Lord, there is hope. There is hope for all, there is hope; (as long as Jesus is alive), yes there is hope."

"Because of the increase of wickedness, the love of most will grow cold, but he who stands firm to the end will be saved" (Matthew 24:12, NIV). Murder, suicide, racism, rape, drug addiction, homelessness, sex and human-trafficking, child molestation, poverty, mass incarceration, mental illness, sickness and disease. The inhumanity across the globe has spoken to the loveless nation we've become. Our understanding of love hasn't penetrated that of our fellow man, only the people we're directly connected to. We hear about these things every day and many of us turn a blind eye because wickedness has become our norm.

We've become like children that grow up in the worst part of town, who have become accustomed to hearing bullets ricochet and hit unintended victims. The IG posts grow old, while the families suffer in silence as their loved ones become another distant memory. Before the blood stains have completely dried, there's another unintended victim. The communities, the parents, the children cry out but who can hear them? Who is listening???!

We forget that none of us are exempt from trials and tribulation. The only thing that can transcend all socioeconomic factors is love. As children of God, we're supposed to bring light to a dark world.

"You are the light of the world. A town built on a hill cannot be hidden. Neither do people light a lamp and put it under a bowl. Instead, they put it on its stand, and it gives light to everyone in the house" (Matthew 5:14-15, NIV).

A nation that doesn't worship the God that created it is doomed! Just as Sodom and Gomorrah were destroyed for idolatry and sexual immorality. Our nation will be destroyed because we refuse to obey the Almighty God. The greatest commandments given to humanity were;

"Love the Lord your God with all your heart and with all your soul and with all your mind. And the second is like it: Love your neighbor as yourself" (Matthew 22:37-39, NIV).

These two commandments show the true heart and nature of God. We live in a nation that has no fear of God and refuses to obey the commandments, that bring life and not death.

The Bible says, in 1Corinthians 13:4-7 "Love is patient, love is kind. It does not envy, it does not boast, it is not proud. It does not dishonor others, it is not self-seeking, it is not easily angered and it keeps no record of wrongs. Love doesn't delight in evil but rejoices with the truth. It always protects, always trusts, always hopes and always perseveres." Love is defined by Webster's dictionary as "strong affection for another arising out of kinship or personal ties". Webster also says that love is "attraction based on sexual desire: affection and tenderness felt by lovers." The world's definition of love is completely different from that of the Bible. The Bible teaches us that love is selfless and is not a feeling or sexual desire but comes from the love of the Almighty God. We've endorsed the Webster's definition of love but not the Bible's. That idea is too complex for many, whom refuse to obey the greatest commandments given to man from the Almighty God.

True love transcends religious customs and doctrine. It's love that prepares the heart to hear the Gospel of Jesus Christ. If you aren't walking in love, you can't show people the love of Christ. The world loves who loves them. But we love because Christ first loved us.

"By this shall all men know that ye are my disciples, if ye have love one to another" (John 13:35, KJV).

If you lack love, you have nothing at all. The world needs more love and that love is only revealed through the children of God. When people know that they're loved they do better. They see themselves in a different light. Love is so powerful because it is the only emotion that can drive out hate.

We say in casual conversation that we love people. When you really love someone the same benefits you have for yourself, you want and work toward for others. The relationship shouldn't dictate the love you have for the individual. That should be something that flows effortlessly through your heart. There are many that speak of the love in their hearts but that love is only expressed in areas of familiarity. When you love, every environment permeates with the love you have.

How can you say you love your fellow man and see him dying or struggling and you turn away? Calamity can strike anyone at any time.

"That ye may be the children of your Father which is in heaven: for he maketh his sun to rise on the evil and on the good, and sendeth rain on the just and on the unjust" (Matthew 5:45, KJV).

The difference between the righteous and the unrighteous is our faith and belief in the Almighty God to calm the storm. As believers and followers of Christ, we're the light of the world. We must show the love of Christ, which resides within us. We can change the evil and wickedness in the world by obeying the commandments and loving the way God wants us to love. It is God's job and His alone to judge the world and people for their sin. Our only job as believers is to show the love of Christ to all. That means you love regardless of political party, race, religious beliefs, gender and or sexual orientation. Everyone you encounter should know you're a child of God because of the love that overflows from your heart.

These are the signs of the times; everyone has become so concerned with themselves and few loves anymore. The world's understanding of love is self-seeking and self-serving. Many have completely left out God and their fellow man. This world lacks humility, which is a major component of love. Love is not loud, destructive, or boastful and doesn't seek to make others feel bad for where they are in life. Love uplifts and builds up. It doesn't tear down. When someone loves you, they see the good in you even when you're in the mud. They fight for you just as much as they fight for themselves.

Love is about sacrificing, so, you can see the greater good in someone else, because you love them. Love doesn't say, you have to change for me to love you. Love meets you right where you are and builds you up. Many of our views of love are distorted, we've never had a real relationship with the Almighty God. When you understand how much God loves you; you will see everyone the way God sees them. When God looks at us, He doesn't see the stain of sin. He sees the finished work of Christ on the cross. When we look at the sacrifice made by God for us to live, we can learn to love everyone the way Christ loved us.

"Greater love hath no man than this, that a man lay down his life for his friends" (John 15:13, KJV).

The flesh is an enemy against things of the spirit. We must not love out of our own flesh but by the spirit and grace given to us by God.

"Every good and perfect gift is from above, coming down from

the Father of the heavenly lights, who does not change like shifting shadows" (James 1:17, NIV).

One of the many gifts God has given us is love. With His mighty hand He created love and light. He gave us the commandments to follow so our hearts would not turn wicked in a world filled with sin. Love in the world has waxed cold and people don't love anymore. You cannot have love or life without God. We as a nation have drawn a line in the sand and have said to God, we don't want you. We have taken God out of everything, our schools, workplace, and homes. We have no fear of the Lord, so we refuse to obey His commandments and the world continues to grow colder. Death and destruction continue to wreak havoc in our land, due to our disobedience. We have placed meaningless idols in God's place and have lost all morality.

We have allowed the enemy to pervert the gift of Love. The world has many believing that love must be earned and not given. But the true nature of love was created by God. God loved us when we were yet sinners and He gave the gift of eternal life to mankind. We have settled for the counterfeit love of the world. Love nowadays in common culture, has been associated with sexual immorality and self-indulgence. The world can't love you, but the people that God has placed in this world can show you the love of God. The true love of God is revealed in His sons and daughters. It may be a kind word or gesture that inspires someone to keep going. You never know the battles people are facing internally.

"For God so loved the world that he gave his only begotten son so that whoever believes in him should not perish but have everlasting life" (John 3:16, KJV).

God loved us when we didn't pray, were unfaithful and deep in our sin. The love of God is everlastings and is not based on performance. The Lord loves us when we are following Him and when we are led astray. "And I am convinced that nothing can ever separate us from God's love. Neither death nor life, neither angels nor demons, neither our fears for today nor our worries about tomorrow—not even the powers of hell can separate us from God's love" (Romans 8:38, NLT).

That means that God's love is everlasting and doesn't have to be earned. It's given freely. The greatest commandments given, commissioned man to love God and love our neighbor as ourselves. We shouldn't expect people to earn our love. This isn't the love; God was referring to in His word. It's not up to us to decide who does and doesn't deserve our love based on our own preconceived notions. God doesn't want us to place false expectations on individuals and make them prove their love. The same way we want and expect the Lord to love us flaws and all, is the same way in which we must love our neighbor.

What if God told you, you had to be perfect for Him to love you? What if He said, we had to earn His love? If God were to place expectations on His love. We would all be doomed, because scripture says, we all fall short of the glory of God. For this reason, grace is given. The same grace given to us by God must be given to our fellow man.

I never really understood the true meaning of love. I thought that loving people would always make me feel good. But understood later that love was not a feeling but a choice. When you make a choice to do something for the betterment of yourself or others, it doesn't always feel good. Sometimes we must do what is uncomfortable because the comfortable way of doing things is incorrect.

Growing up as a middle child, I felt like I always had to work extra hard to be seen. As I grew older, I felt I had to earn people's love. So, I always strived to please people, even when it was physically and emotionally detrimental to my own well-being. The same way I worked to earn people's love, is the same way I expected people to earn my love. I didn't understand and couldn't comprehend the right way to love a person. As a result, I made a lot of wrong decisions and failed to love others and myself the right way. If you treated me well and left no bitterness behind, you had my heart. But the moment the kindness left; I was almost out the door.

I didn't realize it but my love was conditional. I would place unspoken expectations on people. The second they let me down, I would become disappointed and no longer wanted to associate with them. This pattern continued in romantic relationships. My lack of understanding love caused me to become aloof and distant when people didn't meet my expectations. I had a false sense of love based on the relationships; I had experienced in the world.

When I first begin forming a relationship with God. I believed, I had to work towards perfection to earn God's love. I thought I had to get everything right for Him to see me and accept me. The Lord showed me, He didn't love me the way man loved me. He had loved me regardless of what I did or didn't do. Many times, we associate our understanding of the things of God with the relationships that we've had with people. We forget that God's not like man. He's perfect in all his ways. The love God provides is perfect.

"There is no fear in love; but perfect love casteth out fear: because fear hath torment. He that feareth is not made perfect in love" (1 John 4:18).

The love of God is so much different from the love of people. You can't truly understand love or know how to love until you've had an encounter with your Creator. We can't earn God's love; it's given to us without expectation and without the need for us to work toward it. God doesn't expect us to be perfect or do works to receive His love. He loves the sinner, the same way, He loves the saint. God wants you to develop a deeper relationship with him that's built on honesty and trust. He wants us to understand the importance of love without expectation.

There are expectations we place on people that will prevent our love from flowing freely. Love is not telling someone to change for you to love them. God met us right where we were. He didn't tell us to clean ourselves up for Him to love us.

The love of God will set you free in your mind, will and emotions. It provides freedom and liberty; it lets us be the best version of ourselves.

In my prayer closet, I begin to ask the Lord to "teach me to love the way He loved." The love of God teaches us how to love like Him and see people the way he sees them. The Lord was patient with us when we were in our mess. Love requires patience and it will require you to stay in the presence of God to receive the grace you need to exercise patience. God uses the most difficult people to strengthen you for the road ahead. The Lord will send people into your life that are difficult to love, to show you what resides in your heart.

God must remove anything in you that is not like Him. He doesn't do this to frustrate us, He does this to purify us, so we can be more like Him. You must be purged of everything that's not like God in order to be used. God wants us to be free in our emotions, He doesn't want circumstances or people controlling our behavior. When we learn to love like God, we can respect people for who they're without changing them. It's not our job to judge people but only to love them the way God loves us. The Lord loves all His children, He wants the sick, broken, lost and confused to come to Him with everything.

The Lord wants you to experience the fullness of His love. So, you can spread it all over the world. Maybe you've made mistakes in your past or felt that no one in your life has really cared for you. I want you to know that there's a heavenly Father who loves you with an everlasting love. One who sent His only son to die for you, so you can have eternal life.

∞∞∞

Chapter 12: Let Go!

∞∞∞

Letting go is a process that is hard for many of us, but it's necessary for growth. In our youth, we develop preconceived notions and perceptions, that are not always true. God knows in His infinite wisdom; what we need to let go of to inherit the promise. He knows the people, places and mindsets that need to be released. Many times, we don't understand why God pulls us away from people who are closest to us. I didn't understand why everyone and everything that I was so familiar with was changing. I didn't know then, but I know now. When I begin to lose, it opened my eyes to things, I hadn't seen before. I experienced great hurt and lost, but in this process learned valuable lessons. These lessons built a tenacity in me, that continue to push me towards greatness. Death teaches you what life can't, failure teaches you, what success can't. Some of life's most valuable lessons are only learned through pain. Sometimes you have to lose, to win again!!

Great lost exposed dysfunction in my life in a vivid way. I'd been operating in dysfunction for a long-time, without my own knowledge. I would often say in casual conversation, "I felt like I was in limbo, this weird place, I couldn't seem to escape." From the outside looking in, you couldn't see the deep cracks in my foundation. To be honest, I couldn't see them either. I had functioned in this space for so long, that it became my norm.

On June 2, 2017, my life changed forever. I received a call that left me devastated; for the first time in my life, I was at a loss for words. "Dee come to the hospital; it's about your father." I said, "can I speak to him, is he ok?" "Just come to the hospital Dee." I knew at that very moment, he was gone. It didn't matter that I'd spoken to him a few hours ago, or that I promised to visit him the very next day. He was gone and there was no way for me to bring him back. This lost sent me into a deep depression. I didn't have the desire to do anything or speak to anyone. Grief left me breathless; there were moments I felt like I couldn't breathe. I felt deep sorrow and anguish and tried to use the things of the world to numb my pain.

At the time, I had been in a relationship for over four-years and had become complacent. Even though my needs weren't met, I stayed. He was comfortable, he was safe, I found solitude in the idea of him. I also lost sight of any dreams or aspirations, I once had. I worked a job, I hated for over four-years, because the money was good. I couldn't move, I was paralysis, forced to stay in my condition. It was as if, a dark veil kept my eyes covered and I couldn't see my way out.

As the months passed, the Lord began to open my eyes to the dysfunction all around me. You see, He used the pain of losing my father to expose the cracks in my life. He took the great pain I'd experienced and allowed me to gain a valuable perspective and insight. There was no way to bring my father back, but now I could see, what I needed to let go of. To become the woman God created. Death taught me to value life, and how to let go of things and people that no longer suited me.

When I surrendered my life to the Lord, He began to strip me of everything that I once knew. As I begin to lose friendships, relationships, finances and even health. My eyes were opened wider than ever before. During this process I didn't question God, but I still didn't understand the importance of letting go of everything I was so comfortable with.

As I read the book of Job, I felt like my experience in some ways mimicked his. Why was I losing the identity that I was so closely connected to? I didn't know at the time, but God was giving me a new life. He was removing the old and replacing it with the new. The things He was forcing me to let go of, were for my own good. The old environments, people and mindsets, couldn't cultivate the new life. I had to let go of my own preconceived notions and adopt my heavenly Father's.

"I have come to set the world on fire, and I wish it were already burning! I have a terrible baptism of suffering ahead of me, and I am under a heavy burden until it is accomplished. Do you think I have come to bring peace to the earth? No, I have come to divide people against each other! From now on families will be split apart, three in favor of me, and two against or two in favor and three against" (Luke 12:49:52).

The call of God is disruptive, it separates you from everything that you know and are accustomed to. When God begins to orchestrate your life, don't get caught up in the emotions of what you've lost along the way. God requires your obedience and dependency on Him. We must move, when God tells us to move and surrender everything. We sometimes like to give God the comfortable "yes." This is the "yes" that doesn't require us to modify our behaviors or make any changes in our lives. It's impossible for you to stay the same and reach destiny.

In order to move into the things of God, you must go through the process. This process requires isolation and purification. God must begin to qualify our thoughts, actions and environments. He will separate you from anything and anyone that's not pushing you toward your purpose. This can be a career, friendship or relationship. Anything that doesn't speak to your next level must go. There are some lessons we can't learn until we learn to let go of the old and familiar. We can't be afraid of letting go, we must walk fearlessly into our new life.

Alignment is necessary for you to walk in the things of God. The process involves removing the old and replacing it with the new. Every step we take when we're in alignment with God is divinely orchestrated. It's never personal but every relationship in your life must speak to the purposes, that God has called you to. Sometimes God allows you to go through a season of isolation so you can find yourself and build a deeper relationship with Him.

When God removes your people of comfort. He is telling you, that He wants to commune with you and only you. He wants to reveal the promises and purposes; He has for your life.

God uses willing vessels, to manifest His glory on earth. You can receive the prophetic word, but you must take the necessary steps to align your life with the will of God and be obedient. This requires a heart change and full surrender; we must let go of what we think things are supposed to look like. We must learn to operate by faith and not out of fleshly emotions. When you start to see things the way God sees them; you can navigate with a clear head, knowing that God's in control of every step.

When we don't move toward the future, we can find ourselves in desolate places. These places speak to the women we were before Christ. Desolate places can't push us to greatness, and if we aren't careful, they can hinder our growth. In the Bible, in the book of John 5:5, there was a certain man who had an infirmity for thirty-eight years. This man had been around a multitude of people who were sick, blind, lame, paralyzed and waiting by a pool. The condition of this man hadn't changed, because he was surrounded by sick people in a desolate place. It doesn't matter how much you want to succeed and believe in your dreams. You must get around people that are like-minded or you will be stuck like this man. The saying misery loves company is true. People who are sick and unhappy want you to stay there with them. This man had the desire to be healed but because of the environment he placed himself in, he stayed sick. It wasn't until Jesus came and asked him if he wanted to be well that he was able to get up and walk.

Let go of people and environments that keep you stuck. God doesn't allow you to stay the same. He knows the visions and dreams; He has given you need to be cultivated in an environment with people who are well. When God pulls us out of these environments, it's for a purpose. If we want our lives to change, we can't go back to those old environments. Maybe God closed the door on your dream job, because He wants you to start a new business. When we look at lost from the wrong perspective, we can miss the new thing God is trying to bring into our lives.

"Be not deceived: evil communications corrupt good manners" (1Corinthians 15:33, KJV).

God will begin to surround you with people that are kingdom minded. He wants to place you in rooms that will force you to grow and become. The Lord knows the right amount of pressure needed, for you to become the woman, He created. As women of God, we must be intentional with every decision and thought. We have empowered these phrases that are catchy but not accurate such as, "no new friends." There are new purposeful relationships, that will never develop until you let go of old ones. I wouldn't say, I have a bunch of close friends, but I do understand the importance of cultivating new relationships.

When God is elevating the way, you think; you can't afford to be around people that won't see the vision. It's important to surround yourself with like-minded individuals. Any relationship that God places in your life is for a divine purpose. These people will help you get closer to the promises God has for you.

When Mary was told by the angel Gabriel, she would birth our savior, she had to connect her faith to Elizabeth. At the time, Elizabeth was 6 months pregnant with John the Baptist. When Mary greeted Elizabeth, her baby leaped. We must surround ourselves with others that are pregnant with the promises of God, so our babies can continue to leap. If we surround ourselves with individuals without dreams or a vision for their lives, we run the risk of not carrying our promises full-term. Lacking the spiritual maturity to understand, there are some things that must die for us to inherit the promise.

God chooses who He wants in our lives, in every season. It's all according to His plans and purposes. God will begin to remove people, that don't speak to the woman, He is calling you to be. God will introduce new people, when He wants to bless you.

These people teach us valuable lessons for the journey ahead. In many cases, after the lesson is taught these people are suddenly removed. God never intended for us to stay the same. When we're afraid to lose people, we keep ourselves bound and prevent the movement of God in our lives. There are some people, that aren't meant to stay in your life long-term, they're only there for a season.

God didn't intend for everyone that started with you to finish with you. God knows that there are people within our camp, that don't have the capacity to go where we are going. Gideon had a different encounter with God and was called a mighty man of valor. God wanted to use him as a vessel to deliver Israel. Gideon wasn't confident in the task God was calling him to do, so he gathered up thirty-two-thousand men to fight the Midianites.

The Lord said to Gideon, "You have too many warriors with you. If I let all of you fight the Midianites, the Israelites will boast to me that they saved themselves by their own strength" (Judges 7:2-3, NIV).

God knew that Gideon was afraid. But He needed Gideon to trust in Him, not in the men he gathered. The odds had to be stacked up against him, so he would know the battle was won by the Lord. God also knew that all ten-thousand men weren't really going to support Gideon on the journey. Gideon was carrying dead weight. God had to test the men in Gideon's camp, to ensure he was connected to the right people before delivering the Midianites in his hands. When God finished testing all the men, there were only three-hundred left. There are people in our lives that want to be around for the promise but not the pain. God removes the people that won't push you toward greatness, but want to be around to reap the benefits.

God never removes anything you need. So, you can be confident in knowing whatever God is removing it won't assist you in the journey ahead. We, like Gideon, want to be comfortable and want to walk in what's familiar. We bring people along, we know won't help. Because it gives us a false sense of security. God doesn't want you comfortable, He wants you to trust in Him only.

The Lord's desire is to deliver you from old mindsets that have caused you hurt and pain. The enemy of our soul, wants to distort our judgment with old ways of thinking. Old memories and mindsets won't produce good fruit. These places prevent you from grabbing hold of the future God has for you. We must release those old places of hurt, and tell those doubts and fears that they can't live in this space any longer. If we don't evict the old mindsets, we will never reach, our fullest potential. Old mindsets can have you wanting to stay in what's familiar, and hinder your growth. When God begins to heal and restore, you cannot stay stuck in your past hurt. God will surround you with people who have turned their pain into purpose. He doesn't want you to wallow in your past experiences, regrets, and mistakes. God promises to bring restoration and wholeness. He's doing a new thing in your life.

"Behold, I will do a new thing; now it shall spring forth; shall ye not know it? I will even make a way in the wilderness, and rivers in the desert" (Isaiah 43:19, KJV).

When we accept Christ as our Lord and Savior, we inherit eternal life and all the promises that God has for us. "For you died, and your life is now hidden with Christ in God" (Colossians 3:3, NIV). When God rescues us from sin. He gives us a new life, new name, hope, and a future. He doesn't want us to operate in our emotions, focusing on the things He has removed and not the future that's in front of us.

As women walking in purpose, we must walk by faith and not by sight. When we walk by sight, we see things from the fleshly perspective and lack the spiritual maturity to continue the journey. Walking by sight doesn't allow you to see the provisions, God has already made available before the foundations of the earth were formed. It forces you to move based solely on what you see now. Walking by sight hinders you and prevents you from walking in your purpose. Walking by faith, doesn't require us to see the provision but our trust in God enables us to grab a hold of the promise. Walking by faith allows God to reposition our lives for the promise. When our trust is in what we see and not in God, we miss the opportunity and breakthrough.

The new thing requires a different version of yourself. There's new territory, God wants you to be prepared to occupy. God takes you out of situations that don't pull on your intellect. God moves things in your life to make you uncomfortable and force you to grow. God knows that you'll never get to the promise being the same.

Change is inevitable and people that refuse to change stay the same. If you're always around the same people and environments, your knowledge can't develop. You can't wait for people to change; you must move forward and allow them to catchup when they're ready. Comfort can be crippling. It can keep people stuck in unsuccessful friendships, relationships, careers, ministries, and mindsets. Just because it feels right doesn't mean it's right. The past can never tell you your future!! Each obstacle and relationship train us for where, we are going next.

"Remember what happened to Lot's wife" (Luke 17:32, NLT).

Lot and his family resided in Sodom and Gomorrah. God ordered them to flee because He was going to destroy the land. God had plans and a future for Lot and his family, but when his wife looked back, she instantly turned into a pillar of salt. God doesn't want us focusing on the past and what we lost. If we focus on the past, we can never move forward in our future. When we look back at the things of the past, we stay stagnant. Everything God has for us, is in front of us. Looking back at the past, can kill your destiny.

There are some relationships that enter our lives, when we're in a broken place. At one point, we were able to connect with those individuals because of the pain of our past. When the healing process begins, we start to realize, we don't have anything in common. We were connected by the pain and not purpose.

Have you ever had a conversation with someone that was stuck in the past? No matter what good has come in their life. They only see the bad, who left, and who wasn't there. These people can keep you in a cycle of loss by constantly reminding you of their pain. In order to move forward, you must let these individuals go. When we hold on to people God wants us to remove, we're adding excess baggage. As a result, many people find themselves drained. Everyone is not your assignment! God doesn't give you the grace to help everyone. God wants to remove these people for a reason. He knows they will hinder and distract you from your destiny.

Some people in our lives are called to be our Judas in various seasons. The Lord doesn't want us making idols out of any relationship. He will tell you when to let go of certain people to avoid being hurt by them. The Lord needs you to walk by the Spirit and not by the flesh. Anything we can't let go of has become an idol in our lives. Judas was used by the evil one to betray Jesus. If Jesus was too wrapped up in the emotion of the betrayal, He wouldn't have been able to complete His mission and save humanity. Everything the enemy intends for evil God will use for your good. Pain and rejection can help push you to greatness. There are some lessons that can only be learned through pain. To be rejected by man is to be chosen by God. When there is favor on your life, people will be able to see it before you will. They will reject you and you won't understand why. They will try to bury you to keep you from reaching your dreams.

God will allow you to go through a season in your life when you're barren. During these times, He wants you to put all your faith and trust in Him. He doesn't want you relying on material possessions, jobs, people, or money. He wants you to know Him as your provider. When we rely on the things or people of this world, we can be controlled by it. The Lord wants you to depend only on Him. If the loss of these things makes you crumble, you will know where you have placed your trust. God's desire is never to see you without, but He must purify all your motivations. When you don't have any safety nets, your true heart towards God is revealed.

In the barren place, God will also reveal the hearts of the people closes to you. It's easy for people to say they have your back when you don't need anything from them. But when you're in the low place, He opens your eyes and exposes their true intentions. Although this process is painful, it's needed before you move to the next level. Everyone can't go, there are some that you need to let go of. God wants you to know the people that you connect yourself with aren't always good for you.

God's always calling us out of the familiar, so we can experience the supernatural. When Jesus chose His disciples, they were already in a career that they had mastered. Jesus called them out of what was comfortable, so He could prepare them to walk in their purpose. Jesus told Peter, "I will make you a fisher of men". Peter was comfortable catching fish, but he had no experience fishing for men. Jesus called him to something new, that challenged him to drop his nets. God is always encouraging us, to step out on faith, so He can do a new thing in our lives.

∞ ∞ ∞

∞∞∞

"Whatever you do, do well. For when you go to the grave, there will be no work or planning or knowledge or wisdom" (Ecclesiastes 9:10 NLT).

There was a time, I would go out every day. I had to be at the party or the latest events. I always felt like I was missing out on something. As I look back, I can see how my lack of discipline allowed me to stay stuck in the same place for years. I wasn't out celebrating success and hard work. I had an idle mind and needed to be entertained. The saying is true "an idle mind is the devil's playground". The enemy will use your lack of discipline to keep you distracted and from reaching your goals. If your mind is not set and focused on the things of God, time will get away from you. To walk in purpose, you must be intentional and understand that time is your most valuable asset.

God's the only one in the universe who's not bound by time. He's the Creator of time and seasons. However, God values time more than we know. He wants us to understand the importance of valuing our time here on earth. Everyone, regardless of age, race, gender, financial status, and or religious beliefs are given the same 24 hours per day. Time is considered a limited resource because once it's gone. It's gone forever. It doesn't matter how rich or smart you are, you can never buy back or outsmart your way into receiving more time.

"Teach us to number our days, that we may gain a heart of wisdom" (Psalm 90:12, KJV).

My mother used to tell me when I was a little girl, how quickly time would fly. When I became upset with her; I would always say, "I can't wait 'till I'm grown." When you're a kid, you think you have forever! I didn't understand the importance of time until I reached adulthood. I let environments and people keep me distracted from my purpose. The environments I found myself in didn't cultivate the woman God was calling me to be. I spent time doing things that wouldn't benefit me long-term. I lacked the drive and discipline to fulfill goals that were important to me.

Time is considered our most valuable resource. It must be spent doing things that will edify us spiritually and mentally. Time and discipline go hand and hand and must be built up like a muscle. To be effective, we must organize our days and be mindful of the time spent doing meaningless activities. Meaningless activities are anything that takes you away from your divine purpose.

Take a moment and think about your day-to-day activities. Identify behaviors that will be beneficial to your future. How much time do you spend watching TV? How much time do you spend working at a job you hate? How much time do you spend working on the idea God has given you? How much time do you spend in the presence of God?

You must be mindful of the moments you spend not being productive. Ask God to divinely orchestrate your steps and keep you from idle activities, so you can bear fruit in every season. When we effectively allocate our time, we're more efficient. When we lack discipline. We allow instant gratification to keep us bound. We won't move forward with the steps toward change, because we aren't comfortable with the process.

The transformation process requires a renewing of your mind. The process of dying daily isn't pretty. God must take you through the fire, so you can be purified. Full transformation requires you to get uncomfortable and move by the leading of the Holy Spirit. We can pray all we want but if we don't change our habits, nothing changes.

A part of taking up your cross and dying daily is denying yourself the instant gratification, so, you can see the bigger picture. If you never deny yourself, you lack the discipline to perform with accuracy. God can't fully move through you, because you are unable to discipline your flesh. God's in search of willing vessels that will submit to His authority. If we want to be used by God, we must have a willing, surrendered heart.

There are ideas inside you, that need to be birthed. When we embrace who God has called us to be, we can birth ideas that can change the world. God gives good gifts to His children; He wants you to serve those gifts to the world. This requires managing your time and resources, so the promise can be manifested in your life.

"A man's gift opens doors for him and bringeth him before great men" (Proverbs 18:16, KJV).

We're responsible for taking the practical steps to achieve our goals. God isn't going to send you the opportunity of your dreams, without you taking the steps to prepare. Opportunity must meet preparation. You must make room for the blessings you're asking God for. "I have observed something else under the sun. The fastest runner doesn't always win the race, and the strongest warrior doesn't always win the battle. The wise sometimes go hungry, and the skillful are not necessarily wealthy. And those who are educated don't always lead successful lives. It is all decided by chance, by being in the right place at the right time" (Ecclesiastes 9:11, NLT).

Lack of discipline can keep you bound in your mind, will and emotions. God can't bring prosperity into your life, without you developing successful habits. The decisions that we make regarding our time can either help or hinder us. We have grown accustomed to having everything at our fingertips and anything that requires hard work, we bail on. It's important to invest in the person you want to become, by creating behaviors that change the way you think and use your time. If you get lazy in the process, you will never inherit the promise.

We must invest in the person we want to be in the future, not the person we are now. If God has told you to start a business, write a book, or pursue a new career, take the time to invest in something new. Be disciplined enough to learn a new skill. God will give you the ideas and talent, but it's up to you to take the steps necessary to learn a new craft. Discipline requires you to change daily habits to produce a desired outcome. Changing your habits can be difficult at first. It requires a changing of your mind and casting down thoughts that are not from God.

"Casting down imaginations, and every high thing that exalteth itself against the knowledge of God, and bringing into captivity every thought to the obedience of Christ" (2Corinthians 10:5, KJV).

Every action has a reaction. If you make the decision to be proactive, instead of reactive. You will reposition your mindset to handle any season that may come your way. When God gives us a vision, we're responsible for partnering with Him to manifest it on earth. The word God gives us must become flesh. It already exists in the spirit but God partners with us, so heaven can come to earth.

"The word became flesh and made his dwelling among us We have seen his glory, the glory of the one and only Son, who came from the Father, full of grace and truth" (John 1:14, NIV).

It's our job to apply the spiritual principles given to us by God, so, the promise can physically manifest on earth. When we get into the habit of making the best decisions for ourselves every day; we put the vision God has given us ahead of what, we may see now. This requires us to develop the strategy and specific goals needed to reach the place God has prepared for us. Ask yourself every day, does my decisions align with where I want to be?

Let go of those thoughts that tell you, you can't or aren't good enough. Think about the decisions you've made within the last two-three years. How have these decisions effected your life? If they haven't affected your life in a positive way. Change the trajectory of your life, by making positive strives to discipline yourself and manage your time wisely.

∞∞∞

∞∞∞

"I freed a thousand slaves; I could have freed a thousand more if only they knew they were slaves."
-Harriet Tubman

Some of our ancestors have never been enslaved; while others have been physically and systematically oppressed. Many of us believe we're far removed from slavery; but you can be enslaved so long that you forget you're a slave. I'm not referring to the history of slavery among African Americans, but the bondage of oppression the world has placed on all of us regardless of ethnicity. Paul says in Romans 12:2, "Do not conform any longer to the pattern of this world, but be transformed by the renewing of your mind. Then you will be able to test and approve what God's will is – his good, pleasing and perfect will."

When you give your life to Christ; you're abandoning the systems of this world and entering the Kingdom of Heaven. Satan keeps people ensnared by the attractiveness of the things of this world such as; money, power and other worldly desires. "The god of this age has blinded the minds of unbelievers, so that they cannot see the light of the gospel of the glory of Christ, who is the image of God" (2 Corinthians 4:4). The enemy controls people through the enslavement of their minds. "For as he thinketh in his heart, so is he" (Proverbs 23:7, KJV). The battlefield has always been in the mind, this tactic has been used by the enemy to control people since the beginning of time.

To keep you in the mindset of a slave, the slave master's tricks are very crafty. He uses psychological warfare to keep you stuck in a slavery mentality, so you will never escape your condition. Psychological warfare is defined as the deliberate use of various manipulations, promotion, and deceptive techniques, such as spreading propaganda and terror, to induce or reinforce attitudes that are favorable to gain strategic advantages over others. Psychological warfare is very demonic and has been used since the beginning of time to manipulate and control the masses. It was used in World War II to manipulate soldiers into thinking their wives were cheating. Adolf Hitler used it to appear God-like, he used radios, microphones, and charged rhetoric to indoctrinate youth.

Some of the tactics the enemy of our soul uses; is fear, confusion, and demoralization, among others. He uses fear and the familiarity of your surroundings to make you afraid to step into the unknown. This technique keeps you from occupying the new land and keeps you stuck in old relationships, opportunities, and in constant survival mode. The enemy knows, if he can invoke enough fear, you will be afraid to trust God and step out on faith. The other tactic used by the enemy is confusion, He will mix the truth with a lie, to frustrate you and encourage you to give up, or believe you aren't hearing from God. The enemy knows, if he can feed you enough lies about yourself or the new place. You won't be confident in your ability to occupy the land and you will be afraid to step out on faith. Another tactic used by the enemy is demoralization. He will use your environment, your past and words spoken against you, to break you down. He wants you to believe that you aren't worthy or able to do the things that God has called you to do.

Satan's goal is to keep you enslaved and in bondage to the systems of this world. He doesn't want you to have the mind of Christ, he wants you to believe his lies. The Israelites wandered in the wilderness for forty-years; during this time God was teaching them to put their trust only in him. When we put all our trust in God, He can do the miraculous in our lives. God needed to remove the slavery mentality from them before entering the Promised Land.

"Then it came to pass, when Pharaoh let the people go, God did not

lead them by way of the land of the Philistines, although that was near; for God said, 'Lest perhaps the people change their minds when they see war, and return to Egypt.' So, God led the people around by way of the wilderness of the Red Sea. And the children of Israel went up in orderly ranks out of the land of Egypt" (Exodus 13:17-18, KJV).

God took them a different way, so they could gain confidence in moving to the new place. God wanted to test them and improve their character, to make sure they would obey in the Promised Land. The Israelites had been in Egypt for four-hundred and thirty years, and had been victims of psychological warfare. It didn't matter that they were free physically; they were still in bondage in their minds. The Lord knew, if they entered the new land with that old mindset, the new blessings would kill them.

They needed to learn the strategies needed to be fruitful in the Promised Land. The Israelites were enslaved in Egypt by Pharaoh. They had become comfortable with the lifestyle of a slave and didn't know how freedom looked or felt. They were oppressed for so long, that they had forgotten how to trust only in God. God wanted them to know Him as their provider. He protected them in the wilderness and provided all their needs. He allowed them to be hungry and then fed them with manna. He needed them to know "man doesn't live by bread alone, but by every word that comes from the mouth of the Father." Their feet never swelled because their shoes and clothes grew with them. If we aren't obedient and don't hearken to the voice of the Lord. We miss the opportunity for God to make the adjustments needed for us to become women, who are prepared for the Promise Land.

God's all-seeing and all-knowing; He knows everything you will encounter in the new land. He wants you to be prepared to fully possess the land and that requires obedience. When we're obedient, God can realign our lives and attitudes. This ensures we're ready to grab hold of the promise. God requires our full obedience in order to step into new territory. When you're obedient, God can give you divine strategies to be fruitful in your new land.

Everyone's Promised Land is different, because no one has the same destiny. Your Promised Land can be a new marriage, business, ministry or career opportunity. Whatever that area maybe, God has to prepare you for the new thing. God doesn't want you reverting to what's familiar. He wants you to be prosperous in the new place. We don't know the way God wants us to take, but He does.

When you're a slave to the systems of this world, you operate based on the world's timetable. When you're a servant of the Lord, every step is divinely orchestrated by God. The new territory, the new people, and the new environments are scary. It requires you to step out on faith and trust that God has prepared you for every obstacle, you will encounter. If you're afraid to embrace new people, new environments, and new opportunities, you will never be able to enter your Promised Land. You will be afraid of the new and will always revert to the old. When we get into alignment with God, He can remove everything we don't need in our new land.

The doors you want God to open can be unlocked by your obedience. Everything that God gives you comes with responsibility. God will give you ideas that come directly from His throne room. These ideas are things He wants manifested on earth, to establish the Kingdom of Heaven.

The Lord takes you through the wilderness to free you of the mindsets that keep you bound and enslaved. So, when you step into the Promised Land, you aren't afraid to grab hold of the new place. This requires a different work ethic and a behavior change that's different from Egypt. In Egypt, you were enslaved and forced to do the work of Pharaoh to build his kingdom. You were treated as slaves and in bondage with no way of escape. The Lord with His mighty hand, set you free, so you can step into your purpose and advance the Kingdom of God.

Whatever you're asking God for you must be prepared to receive. Everything God does is in decency and order; He doesn't operate out of confusion. He will never give you something, He knows you will not be able to manage. If you're unable to manage what He's currently giving you, then He will not give you more.

We must partner with God to manifest the blessing. God will move the mountains that need to be move for us to get to our expected end. But we must work to maintain the weight God is trusting us with. This requires discipline, consistency, and hard work. To develop a muscle, you must work out repeatedly to receive results. The new territory God is providing requires a different mentality. It consists of working when you want to sleep, staying in while everyone else is out having fun. You can't afford to binge watch your favorite show for eight hours or be frivolous with your spending. The only way to withstand the weight that will be placed on you is through consistency and discipline. God will begin to change your habits and surrounding so you're ready to move to the next level of your destiny.

The mentality of a man is very important, the mind can keep him imprisoned. He will be afraid to dream beyond what he sees. He will only be able to envision his circumstances. "For as he thinketh in his heart, so is he" (Proverbs 23:7, KJV).

God wants to deposit mindsets, strategy and ideas that will wonder the world. If you're too afraid to step into the next dimension. You will never be able to grab a hold of your blessings. The old saying goes "you can lead a horse to water but you can't make him drink." The horse must be thirsty enough to lean down and drink.

Utilize every opportunity God's placing in your life. Don't look at your past mistakes, failures or the old way of thinking. Step into the new mindset God is birthing in you. When negative thoughts flood your mind, you must replace them with words that affirm, who God says you are. Believe in yourself and be confident in the

Almighty God. When you stand in that confidence. You know, no matter what may come, God's in control. You will be steadfast, unmovable and unshakeable; walking fearlessly in your divine purpose.

"Therefore, my dear brothers and sisters, stand firm. Let nothing move you. Always give yourselves fully to the work of the Lord, because you know that your labor in the Lord is not in vain" (1 Corinthians 15:58, NIV).

God is creating a different version of you. Yield to the process! When you step into the next dimension, know that God is aligning every step, so, you can reach your destiny. God doesn't want you to operate out of fear. He wants you to be confident in who He is calling you to be. He wants you to be bold and fearless and ready to take on the world. He wants to use you as a vessel so His glory can be revealed on earth.

There's a process to elevation and it requires isolation and separation. God separates you from everything you know and have learned in Egypt. To become the woman God wants you to be you must operate and function in a different capacity.

When God's elevating your life, it's important to watch the company you keep and your environment. God tests everyone connected to you, to show you who to take on the next step of your journey. Every friend isn't connected to the destiny God has for you. You will have to separate from some people because you're going down two very different paths. Everyone can't go with you to your Promised Land. It may be hard because you want to take your friends and family but it will only prevent them from fulfilling the destiny that God has for them.

It's important to make sure that everyone you're connected to has a heart for God. If you have someone in your circle that isn't loyal, he or she can corrupt what God wants to do in your life. In the Bible, God told Joshua that he would win the battle against AI. God told him that everything in Jericho belonged to

Him and had to be destroyed. But Achan disobeyed the Lord and stole a Babylonian robe, two hundred pieces of silver, and a gold bar. Because he disobeyed the Lord, Joshua lost the battle to the Amorites and Achan had to be put to death. The saying is true "one rotten apple can ruin the bunch." As you move forward and align yourself with the purposes of God, don't be afraid to lose people. There are people that must be removed for you to inherit the promise. A huge part of the realigning process, is allowing God to remove the people that aren't going into your next season.

"So, the Lord said to Joshua, Get up! Why is it that you have fallen on your face? Israel has sinned; they have also transgressed My covenant which I commanded them to keep. They have even taken some of the things under the ban, and they have both stolen and denied the theft. Moreover, they have also put the stolen objects among their own things. This is why the solders of Israel could not stand and defend themselves before their enemies; they turned their backs and ran before the, because they have become accursed. I will not be with you anymore unless you destroy the things under the ban from among you" (Joshua 7:10-12, AMP).

When you align your vision with the will of God, it requires you to separate yourself and the way you see the vision. There are environments and people that won't speak to the vision. Make the decision to remain focused on the vision.

When God is realigning your life with purpose. He shows you, the gifts and talents He has given you. You may have never considered yourself a great speaker, but God will open doors for you to do speaking engagements. God knows all the treasures He has placed down on the inside of you. He wants you to trust Him, so He can begin to physically manifest, what you can't see. It's never about who you are now. It's about the person God is calling you to be in the process, each piece plays an important role in your development. Don't bury your gifts.

"After a long time, their master returned from his trip and called them to give an account of how they had used his money. Then the

servant with the one bag of silver came and said, Master, I knew you were a harsh man, harvesting crops you didn't plant and gathering crops you didn't cultivate. I was afraid I would lose money, so I hid it in the earth. Look, here is your money back. But the master replied, you wicked and lazy servant! If you knew I harvested crops I didn't plant and gathered crops I didn't cultivate, why didn't you deposit my money in the bank? At least I could have gotten some interest on it" (Matthew 25:19, 24-27).

The servant in this story was afraid to invest in the gift God had given him. He didn't believe in himself and was afraid to step out on faith. The master wanted the servant to develop what He had given Him. When God is producing new fruit in your life, He wants it to grow. The servant compared his gift to the other servants and became insecure. He decided, based on the others, he didn't have enough in his hand. Because this servant compared his talents to others, it paralyzed him.

When we compare ourselves to other people, we're saying to God "what you have given me isn't enough." Everyone God created is different, there are no duplicates. Comparison diminishes the qualities of both individuals. You can't be so focused on someone else's boat that you drown. It doesn't matter where you find yourself, work on whatever God has given you. Don't compare your progress with anyone else's. When you're building something, you've never seen built, you won't have a blueprint. The only thing you'll have is the vision that God has placed in front of you.

"Do not despise these small beginnings, for the Lord rejoices to see the work begin, to see the plumb line in Zerubbabel's hand" (Zechariah 4:10, KJV).

Don't become consumed with how small your start is. The seed that was planted down on the inside of you will grow when you get into alignment with your heavenly Father. Put your faith in God and trust in the word He has given you. Trust in the word of the Lord when everyone is walking away from you. Trust in the word of the Lord when you're losing everything and the pieces that you thought were coming together seem to be falling apart. The devil will always come after the word God has given you to make you doubt. God wants you to walk by faith and not by sight. If you walk by sight, you will be deceived. You must stand on the word of God when all else fails.

If you don't restructure your life, you will never see the promise manifested. You can unknowingly operate in unbelief. When you operate in unbelief, you won't move when God is telling you to move. You won't believe that God will do it for you. Believing this will keep you from operating in your fullest capacity. You won't change the behaviors that need to be changed for you to birth, everything God has called you to do. When you go back and forth between belief and unbelief, you are inconsistent in your thought process.

The Bible says, in James 1:8, that a "double minded man is unstable in all his ways." When you are double minded you can expect nothing from God because your beliefs are divided. This will produce inconsistency and you won't work toward the promise. When we believe God for something, we begin the preparation so we can receive the blessing. If you're just waiting for the promised to manifest without the work, then you're not moving by faith. Faith without works is dead!! The faith that we have in the promised pushes us to work toward it. When you know that God is capable and able, you prepare even when you don't see the provision. When you prepare without the provision, you're showing God that no matter what the situation looks like. I will trust you. In this, you're exercising perfect faith. The circumstances surrounding you don't matter; God can change your life with one blessing. When you pray, ask God to restore your faith in the promises you can't see.

When you're in an unfamiliar place, work to become the best version of yourself. Take the opportunity to learn new things about yourself and other people. Take the time to invest in a fitness regimen and develop a healthy diet. Ask God to help you work on improving yourself, so you can serve the best part of you to the world. God wants you to walk into the newness that He's bringing into your life. He wants you to take the steps necessary to think differently. When John the Baptist said, "Repent for the Kingdom of Heaven is at hand," he is telling us to change our minds. This involves changing the way you see things and operate. Realigning your thoughts with the thoughts of heaven requires you to think and meditate on things that are good and lovely.

"Finally, brothers and sisters, whatever is true, whatever is noble, whatever is right, whatever is pure, whatever is lovely, whatever is admirable-if anything is excellent or praiseworthy- think about such things" (Philippians 4:8, NIV).

In order to be effective, take inventory of where you are and where you're going. If you're only focused on where you want to be, then you will lose sight of the vision and the plan to get there. "Write the vision and make it plan" (Habakkuk 2:2 KJV). Develop a plan and strategy that will help you get to the place God has shown you. Ask God to help you to make the necessary adjustments in your life, so you can see the promise of God manifested.

∞∞∞

∞∞∞

"Greater love hath no man than this, that a man lay down his life for his friends" (John 15:13, KJV).

Institutionalized racism has been embedded in our country since slavery ended. It speaks to the constructs of the prison industry, public health, education, housing and America's wealth gap. It has always been a part of America's fabric, to keep some oppressed and allow others the opportunity to thrive. We take our civil liberties for granted. We have lost sight of the four little girls that lost their lives while attending church in Birmingham, Alabama or the countless lynching's that have plagued our great nation. Many activists and civil rights leaders gave up their freedom and lives; so, we could sit at the front of the bus, vote, live where we want, and go to any restaurant or restroom of our choosing.

The country paints a vivid picture of truth when we think of "Bloody Sunday." We forget that more than fifty-five years ago, many of us were unable to exercise the right to vote in various states in our country. Violence erupted on March 7, 1965 in Selma, Alabama during a peaceful demonstration of approximately six-hundred voting rights advocates; who planned to march from Selma to Alabama. Although African Americans made up more than half of the population, stiff Jim Crow laws significantly reduced the number of registered voters in Dallas county to only two percent. Peaceful demonstrators were met with confederate flags, billy clubs, rubber tubing wrapped in barbed wire and tear gas, as women, children and men were brutally attacked and knocked to the ground. These individuals risked their lives for future generations; many never getting the opportunity to see the change they worked so hard toward.

Let's not forget, the countless others from all races and creeds coming together for a greater good. These people stood up for what was right and were ridiculed by their peers and some put to death. They could have easily turned a blind eye to the suffering of others, but they saw themselves in every individual they fought for.

If you still have a pulse, there's a divine purpose for you here on earth. There's something that's inside of you, that will change the way we think and function in the world. Think about the trail blazers of the past, who historically paved the way, and transformed the way we associate with each other. We know about them today, because they were successful in carrying out their purpose.

Purpose allows you to see, the light at the end of the tunnel is bigger than your pain. When pain has a purpose, it speaks louder than the affliction. If we have the right perspective, we can move forward and liberate someone else through our sufferings. We're all connected; each of us has a key that unlocks another person's breakthrough. God uses our testimonies to empower and strengthen each other's faith. We're not random; we all have a purpose that needs to be manifested on the earth. Our life is not our own, and all the pain is for God's divine purpose.

"But he was wounded for our transgressions, he was bruised for our iniquities: the chastisement of our peace was upon him; and with his stripes we are healed" (Isaiah 53:5, KJV).

God already had a plan to save humanity and it involved Jesus. The bible says, in Revelation 13:8, that the Lamb was slain at the foundation of the earth. The greatest sacrifice ever given was the one made for us, when we were yet sinners. Jesus was crucified, stripped, spat on, beaten, and with nails in His hands and feet, a crown of thorns in His head, He gave His life for mankind. He who had no sin, became sin, to set humanity free. Jesus was the spotless lamb and His sole purpose was to take captive, everything that was holding us back. He was rich, but became poor, so thru

His poverty, we could become rich. His pain had an ultimate purpose, that was bigger than His sufferings.

The Lord doesn't want us to get stuck in the pain. He wants us to push pass the pain and step into our purpose. When we get stuck in the pain, we can't use our sufferings to glorify God. When Jesus was crucified and rose again on the third day, God received all the glory.

In God's eyes, everything is finished. He doesn't live in time, He wrote the end, before He wrote the beginning. Which means, He already has a plan for the pain you've experienced. The pain is the bridge, that connects you to your purpose. God isn't surprised by anything you've been through; He knows the tears you've cried, and uses it for His glory. The pain connects you with the people, that are called to your life. It's through our pain that others are set free. When we use our pain for purpose. We empower both men and women, to not be ashamed of their past, but use it to propel them into their destiny. "They overcame him by the blood of the Lamb and by the word of their testimony" (Revelation 12:11, NIV). The blood of Jesus redeems us and puts us in rightful standing with the Father. We're no longer bound by the pain of the past. But we're able to step into purpose, and use our testimony to glorify God and inspire others.

Many times, we don't understand our sufferings, or the pain we've had to endure. The pain never makes sense, until there is a purpose connected to it. You don't get to choose your ethnicity, gender, economic status, parents, or the neighborhood in which you grew up. God in His sovereignty outlines your life and experiences, so, He can prepare you for your purpose. God is the creator of time and seasons, and every season in your life; prepares you for your purpose. God allows the hurt and pain you've experienced, to push you into your destiny. God always has a purpose for your pain; He uses everything the devil meant for evil, for your good.

When we allow the enemy to use our pain to torment us, we

don't allow God to get the glory from our sufferings. If you've never experienced any suffering in your life, you won't be able to liberate anyone else. The sacrifices we make, aren't just for us, but so others can have freedom both physically and spiritually. Our sacrifices pave the way for future generations and break generational patterns.

God told Abraham to leave his country, family, and everything he knew to go to a place, that God would show him. If Abraham wasn't obedient, he would've stayed in a dry place; a place that did not produce fruit. He would've made the decision to remain in what was comfortable and familiar, and missed out on the promises of God. Abraham made a covenant with God. A covenant is an agreement God makes with His people. God promised great blessings to Abraham's family and his seed. Because of Abraham's covenant, we as his descendants through Christ Jesus, can inherit the promises of God.

God wants to change the way you think and view the world. He wants you to see yourself, the way He sees you. When you begin to see yourself the way God sees you, you can experience life without limitations. You will know that no matter what happens, God loves you. And He's in control of your destiny. Don't be afraid to leave the familiar for the unfamiliar. On the other side of fear is destiny. You'll never be able to experience your unique purpose, until you step out on faith like Abraham.

"For I know the thoughts that I think toward you, saith the Lord, thoughts of peace, and not of evil, to give you hope and a future" (Jeremiah 29:11, KJV).

God uses, the foolish things of this world to confound the wise. In the bible, in the book of Esther, Esther grew up an orphan, but was raised up by God to deliver the Jewish people. Esther didn't know that she would be the one God chose to save the Jews. I'm sure she thought her past and growing up an orphan, would keep her from ever becoming Queen. However, she didn't allow her pain to keep her from moving forward into her destiny. Esther had to be prepared to be the Queen; this required twelve months of purification, prior to meeting the King. She had to step out on faith, not knowing if she would be chosen. The Bible says, King Ahasuerus loved Esther above all the women, and she obtained grace and favor in his sight. Esther didn't know that she would be chosen by the King, but God had already prepared the place. God used her to save her people from being murdered. She had to be obedient and risk her own life to save that of her people.

"For if you remain silent at this time relief and deliverance for the Jews will arise from another place, but you and your father's family will perish. And who knows but that you have come to your royal position for such a time as this" (Esther 4:14, NIV)?

You don't know who's connected to your pain and your obedience. God may tell you to move to a different town or walk away from a friendship or relationship that is no longer beneficial to your growth. He may tell you to start a business or a new ministry; you don't know who may be connected to your "yes". God must prepare you for your destiny. The place is already prepared! God has promises and plans for each of His children. We must be willing to move into unfamiliar territory. God always has a plan and a purpose for the pain. We can't be afraid to move when God says move.

When we realign our lives with God, we can produce fruit in every season. There are habits and actions, we were able to do in previous seasons of our lives, that won't work in the new season. If we want the promised to physically manifest, it will take work. We must work consistently, and never give up on the promise, God has placed in front of us.

When we serve our gift to the world, we empower other people to step into what God has called them to do. Don't be afraid to speak up and allow your voice to be heard. If God has placed you in the room, know you belong there. God has given you the gifts and talents, to stay in the room. Trust God and move when He is telling you to move. It's just a matter of time before you see the physical manifestation of everything that God is calling you to.

God needs a willing vessel and our obedience to follow Him, no matter what we encounter. In life, there are different paths we can take. You can live a mediocre life or the life God wants you to live. God has a plan "A" life that He wants you to grab a hold of. He doesn't want you to settle for plan "B", which is the life you create with your own hands. His desire is for you to step into the destiny, He has for you. There are treasures that your heavenly Father has stored up, just for you. He must prepare you, for the doors He wants you to walk through. This starts with managing the time you spend on things that are not feeding your soul. How much time do you spend on social media? How much time do you spend around people that don't see your vision or have a vision for their own life?

"Every branch that does not bear fruit the Lord removes and every branch that beareth fruit, he purgeth it, that it may bring forth more fruit" (John 15:2).

God wants you to bear fruit in every season of your life; He knows there are some things that need to be cut away. The pruning process can be painful but it's necessary for your growth. God always gives us a choice in following Him, or choosing our own destiny. When we surrender our will for His, He can give us a new life. The pain you've endured in your past was for a divine purpose. The King of Kings placed you in that environment not to kill you but to make you stronger. Everything in your life has been divinely orchestrated by God. The Lord placed you in that family, neighborhood and career, so you can learn from the environment and bring about solutions.

The pain is fertilizer for the promise. It's never easy, but it's necessary to become the women, God wants us to be. We can't afford to stay stuck in the memories of the pain. We're not victims or slaves to our past pains. We must break free, so others can come behind us. The enemy of our soul convinces us to fill the void with temporary idols such as; relationships, drugs, alcohol, sex, material possessions, title, and status among other things. These things feel good for the moment, but they can and will cause a lifetime of pain. When we use the things of this world to cope, we're running from the root issues of the pain.

God wants us to worship Him in spirit and in truth. When Jesus encountered the Samaritan woman at the well, He asked her for a drink. She didn't understand why a Jew was asking a Samaritan for a drink. Jesus was trying to get her to understand and recognize that He wasn't just an ordinary man but He was the Messiah. He also wanted her to recognize that she was thirsty and needed Living Water. He wanted her to be truthful about the idols she had placed in her life. Jesus wanted her to replace them with Living Water.

"Jesus saith unto her, Go, call thy husband, and come hither: The woman answered and said, I have no husband. Jesus said unto her, thou hast well said, I have no husband: For thou hast had five husbands; and he whom thou now hast is not thy husband: in that saidst thou truly" (John 4:16-18, KJV).

He wanted her to know, that He was the Living Water which would provide everlasting life. "But whosoever drinketh of the water that I shall give him shall never thirst; but the water that I shall give him shall be in him a well of water springing up into everlasting life" (John 4:14, KJV). He wanted the truth from her, not who she pretended to be. God can't heal the version of ourselves that we pretend to be; He can only heal the real us. He wants us to identify the things we have used to replace the Living Water in our lives.

Jesus didn't speak about the five husbands to shame this woman. He knew she was in pain. He wanted her to recognize, that she had five husbands, but none of them had been able to quench her thirst, and the one she was with still had her at this well. When we're not honest with God, He can't heal the real us. After the Samaritan woman's honest encounter with Jesus, she was ready to step into her purpose. She gave her testimony of her encounter with Jesus and was able to use her pain to bring others to Christ. She no longer needed the water pot that she had brought to the well because she had received Living Water.

"The woman then left her water pot, and went her way into the city, and saith to the men, Come, see a man, which told me all things that ever I did: is not this the Christ? Then they went out of the city, and came unto him" (John 4:28-30, KJV).

In order to step into purpose, we must be honest about our pain. What idols have you replaced with the Living Water? The things that are holding you back from a real encounter with God. God is spirit, so you don't need to be in a church setting to receive the Living Water. God can meet you right where you are but it requires an honest encounter, so He can heal those broken areas and reveal your identity. Allow Him to use your pain for purpose like He did with the Samaritan woman. God was able to use her testimony to bring other people in her town to believe. I'm sure people must have thought, if this woman can change. It's possible for me. God always has a purpose for the pain!

God wants us to fall in love with the purposes He has for our lives. He wants us to be able to identify anything that doesn't align with that purpose. God will give you the spirit of discernment so you're aware of people and situations that aren't purposeful. He doesn't want us to be enamored by the things or people of this world.

"But seek ye first the kingdom of God and his righteousness and everything will be added to you" (Matt 6:33, KJV).

When we begin to align ourselves with the will of God, He will birth new passions in us. He knows the desires of our heart, He put them there. We can't escape the purposes of God for our lives; they are a part of who we are.

Nothing will be able to satisfy you in this world but God and the purpose, He has called you to. The enemy wants us to be fearful of the new identity and the unfamiliar territory. But Jesus said, "Take heart! I have overcome the world" (John 16:33, KJV). Our heavenly Father has already overcome every obstacle that's placed in front of us —sickness, death, poverty, and depression. There is nothing too hard for our God!

If you never change your perspective, you can become a victim. You must see yourself beyond the pain of your past. The experience has passed, but the lesson can encourage another person. The power of a testimony is so important because it helps another individual to see their problems aren't bigger than God. When we believe our problems are bigger than God. We take the problem from God and put it on our own shoulders. We don't allow God to work the situation out and rest in the peace, that He provides.

"Come to me, all you who are weary and burdened, and I will give you rest. Take my yoke upon you and learn from me, for I am gentle and humble in heart, and you will find rest for your souls. For my yoke is easy and my burden is light" (Matthew 11:28-30, NIV).

God controls every season in our lives. He places us in difficult circumstances not for us to fail, but to make us stronger. He wants us to be able to thrive in any environment. So, He allows opposition to come, so you have no choice but to lean on and trust only in Him. He has a reason that is beyond your level of understanding for your suffering. He wants you to reach inside that pain and pull out the woman who's an overcomer!

Overcome your past, pain, failures, regrets and the lies the enemy tells you about yourself. Our heavenly Father wants you to leave the past behind and walk into your destiny. The pain is creating a fearless woman, who's ready to take on new territory. Get back up!! Don't let the circumstances surrounding your life, keep you down. Speak life over yourself, you were made with a divine purpose in mind.

"For you created my inmost being; you knit me together in my mother's womb. I praise you because I am fearfully and wonderfully made" (Psalm 139:13-14).

There's a freedom in knowing that God is for you, and will never leave you. Tap into the beauty God has for your life. If you aren't sure of your gifts or passions, ask God to reveal them to you. It will require denying yourself, stepping out on faith, and being obedient to the voice of the Father. Begin your mornings and end your nights seeking God's perfect will for your life. Allow God to get the glory from your pain. Let Him use you as His beacon of light. Say "yes" to the will and way of the Lord and His plans for your life.

God's desire is for you to be the head, not the tail, above and not beneath, the lender and not the borrower. When we settle for the mediocre, we settle for less than God's best for our lives. God gives His children good gifts. He wants us to serve those gifts to the world. There are solutions He has placed in you, before the beginning of time. Only you have the grace and capacity to carry out your purpose.

We must get in the presence of God and find our identity. God hasn't created any duplicates; we all have our own DNA and unique gifts. What are those dreams you are too afraid to reach? What are those outlandish ideas, that you still consider possible, even though no one else can seem to understand? Follow the passions that God has placed in you.

Maybe it's fashion, music, dance, acting, accounting, writing, entrepreneurship, or counseling? Whatever passion God has placed on the inside of you, there is a promise connected to it. The Kingdom of God needs to be in every industry. We are the light of the world. When we enter an environment, we bring the light of God with us.

∞ ∞ ∞

∞∞∞

———

"See, I am doing a new thing! Now it springs up; do you not perceive it? I am making a way in the desert and streams in the wasteland" (Isaiah 43:19, NIV).

The Creator of the universe is creating a shift in the atmosphere that is giving you the grace to step out on faith. When God makes you uncomfortable, He is pushing you to grow and do something new. We can't look at every negative experience in our lives from the perspective of the world. God is sovereign, and He will use every negative situation for your good. When we have the right perspective, we can grow from every lesson. Many times, God puts us in difficult circumstances to force us to step out on faith. He knows the environment needed to cultivate the gift that is inside of you. You can't be afraid to fail; failure is the soil needed for success. Every successful person you see and admire today, at some point may have wanted to give up based on their current conditions. We know these individuals because they stayed the course no matter what occurred. Don't look at your reality, have expectations for the future you want to have. Allow yourself to dream again and pursue that dream with passion.

"So, make yourself an Ark of cypress wood; make rooms in it and coat it with pitch inside and out" (Genesis 6:14, NIV). "I am going to bring floodwaters on the earth to destroy all life under the heavens, every creature that has the breath of life in it. Everything on earth will perish" (Genesis 6:17, NIV).

I'm sure Noah must have looked foolish, building an Ark with no rain in sight. But he didn't let the environment dictate his actions. He prepared, based on a word he received from the Lord, and didn't allow anything to knock him off course. He didn't look at his reality; he had great faith and trusted in the word of the Lord. Noah didn't walk by sight; he walked by faith and he and his family were saved when the great flood came.

Many times, we let our environment dictate our actions and don't prepare for what's to come. Build!! Don't worry about what you see today prepare for tomorrow. Don't trust in your own strength or ability, trust in the Lord. Allow Him to show you, how to build based on His specifications.

"I can do all things through Christ who strengthened me" (Philippians 4:13, KJV).

Our heavenly Father allows the opposition, because He doesn't want us to grow arrogant and think that we are doing things within our own strength. He wants us to develop discipline and a work ethic, so no matter what may occur, we are always walking by faith and not by sight. God calls us to commune with Him in the secret place, so He can tell us about things to come and give us greater revelation that will increase our faith. When you believe the word and promises of God, you prepare for the blessing.

"For unto whomsoever much is given, of him shall be much required" (Luke 12:48, KJV).

God will multiply the fruit of thy hands. But if thy hands aren't producing fruit. What is there to multiply? If you give out more love, you get more love. If you sow a seed of grace, you will receive more grace. If you sow seeds of financial blessings, you get more financial blessings. When God opens a new door, He will provide you with the insight and wisdom needed to function in the new environment. It's up to you, to grab hold of everything He's introducing to you. God will give you the idea to create and guide you throughout the process but it will require you to die to the things you're comfortable with to produce something new. God can give you the child. But if you lack the discipline and patience to raise the child up the right way, you will regret when he or she gets older.

Any vision God gives you, is big and will require you to partner with Him to accomplish it. When you put all your trust in God, you're denying your flesh. You're allowing the things that are carnal to die. Whatever you trust in will become your God. If you trust in money, money will become your God. If you trust in men, men will become your God. If you trust in a job, that job becomes your God. Our God is a jealous God and He doesn't like you putting things and people before Him. Anything you put before God is a form of idolatry. Those things must die in you, so you can move freely in the things of God.

You must trust God more than you trust your bank account. Sight says, "I only have this amount of money so I have to save it." Faith says, "my heavenly Father will supply all of my needs according to His riches in glory." When we put our faith and trust back in Him, we show God that we believe He is bigger than any problem we have. We must operate by faith and not by sight. Your fleshly nature must die, so you can get to your destination.

If those things don't die, you will always be afraid of loss. You will always have a lack mentality, and always feel like you don't have enough to accomplish the things God calls you too. You won't walk by faith; you will always walk by sight. Walking by sight will keep you paralyzed and stuck in your current conditions.

You will always be thinking. What if this doesn't work? What if I fail? What if nobody likes my idea? When good opportunities come your way. You will self-sabotage, not believing it's possible for you. You will run away from everything that makes you happy, and run toward the things that hurt you. Walking by sight keeps you focus on what you have in the natural and not the kingdom resources that are available to you. God must remove that mindset, and it requires you to trust Him.

"There is no fear in love. But perfect love drives out fear, because fear has to do with punishment. The one who fears is not made perfect in love" (1John 4:18, NIV).

Fear keeps so many of us bound and fearful of following our dreams and passions. We are afraid to tell our stories because we fear rejection. We want to be accepted by everyone, so we dumb ourselves down to fit in. We don't step into the fullness of who we are and the purpose God has for our lives. Fear keeps us in our place of comfort and from moving forward in the things of God. If you stop allowing fear to tell you, who you are and who you can become. You can become a change agent for the Kingdom of Heaven. God can't move freely in a vessel that's bound by fear. When you remove fear from the equation. You will be fearless, and can produce in a different dimension of faith.

When we understand how much God loves us, we understand everything He does is for our good. The stars will never be perfectly aligned. The conditions will never be perfect. In fact, when you walk by faith, everything will be in a disarray. God needs it to be like that so your faith and trust is only in Him. When God is doing a new thing in your life, and changing the way you think. He must shift everything around you. You will have to produce in uncomfortable seasons. If you don't learn how to produce in your uncomfortable seasons, you will not be able to weather the storms of life.

Sometimes you must crawl through the mud in order to get to the top. The struggle teaches you things privilege never will. The low place makes you look at yourself and begin to assess your ability to be effective in different areas of your life. Hitting rock bottom makes you look in the mirror and get your priorities in order. It provides you with a different level of focus.

When Jesus was on the boat with the disciples while the storms were raging, He was asleep, at peace. There is a peace that the Father gives that surpasses all understanding. The vision God gives you, requires you to be focused and steadfast. God gives you the ability to create but you must believe that God can do it through you.

You can win, God is with you!

"If God is for us, who can be against us" (Romans 8:31, NIV)?

No one can stop what God has for you. You're the only one that can stop the blessings of God due to your own immobility. Step out on faith, live, and be the fearless woman God created you to be!

∞ ∞ ∞

Afterword

If you are not saved, it's never too late to receive salvation. God doesn't expect you to be perfect—He wants you to come to Him just as you are, with all your imperfections. No one knows the hour or the day they will take their last breath. Death does not discriminate against age, race, economic status, or gender. The Bible says in John 14:6, "I am the way, the truth, and the life. No one comes to the Father except through me."

You don't have to be inside a traditional church building to begin your relationship with Christ. God is omnipresent, meaning He is everywhere at the same time. He is with you right now, even as you read this book.

Below is the sinner's prayer. All you need to do is recite this prayer, believe in your heart, and you will be saved. My prayer is that God continues to bless you. I love you—but more importantly, Jesus loves you!

"Dear Lord Jesus, I know that I am a sinner, and I ask for Your forgiveness. I believe You died for my sins and rose from the dead. I turn from my sins and invite You into my heart as my Lord and Savior. Take complete control of my life and help me to walk in Your footsteps daily by the power of the Holy Spirit."

In Jesus' name, Amen.

Amen

∞∞∞